LOVE, MAGIC & MUDPIES

Raising Your Kids to Feel Loved,
Be Kind, and Make a Difference

LOVE, MAGIC & MUDPIES

Raising Your Kids to Feel Loved,
Be Kind, and Make a Difference

By
Bernie Siegel, MD
best-selling author of *Love, Medicine & Miracles*

Notice

This book is intended as a reference volume only, not as a medical manual. The information given here is designed to help you make informed decisions about your health. It is not intended as a substitute for any treatment that may have been prescribed by your doctor. If you suspect that you have a medical problem, we urge you to seek competent medical help.

Mention of specific companies, organizations, or authorities in this book does not imply endorsement by the publisher, nor does mention of specific companies, organizations, or authorities imply that they endorse this book.

Internet addresses and telephone numbers given in this book were accurate at the time it went to press.

Rodale books may be purchased for business or promotional use or for special sales. For information, please write to: Special Markets Department, Rodale, Inc., 733 Third Avenue, New York, NY 10017

Printed in the United States of America

Rodale Inc. makes every effort to use acid-free ♾, recycled paper ♻.

The poem "Purple" on page 127 is reprinted with permission of Alexis Rotella. Copyright © 1983 by Alexis Rotella. All rights reserved.

Book design by Drew Frantzen

Library of Congress Cataloging-in-Publication Data

Love, magic & mudpies: raising your kids to feel loved, be kind, and make a difference/by Bernie Siegel.
    p.   cm
ISBN-13 978-1-59486-554-1 hardcover
ISBN-10 1-59486-554-X hardcover
    1. Child psychology.   2. Child rearing.   3. Love.   I. Title.
HQ772.S493 2006
649'.1—dc22   2006026509

Distributed to the book trade by St. Martin's Press

2   4   6   8   10   9   7   5   3   1   hardcover

We inspire and enable people to improve their lives and the world around them

For more of our products visit **rodalestore.com** or call 800-848-4735

DEDICATION

This book is dedicated to the memory of my parents, Simon and Rose Siegel. It isn't easy to no longer have them as my parents. Being their child was an incredible gift.

I want to do more than thank all those who have continued to give me life, parent me, and raise me to be a decent human being, but I cannot find the words to tell them what I am feeling. My gratitude goes beyond language to my beloved wife—Bobbie, our children and their spouses—Jonathan and Judy, Jeffrey, Stephen and Marcia, Carolyn and Roy, Keith and Jane—and their children, Sam, Gabe, Eli, Simone, Jarrod, Patrick, Jason, and Charlie.

And thank you also to the people who have shared their lives with me over the years in my work as a physician and life coach as we have faced life's difficulties and our mortality and the will to live. I have truly learned from them how to be a survivor, the powerful role parenting plays in our lives, and how we can all be re-parented and reborn.

CONTENTS

PART ONE: ALL IN THE FAMILY—FAMILY LIFE AND VALUES

Part Two: Love Is the Main Ingredient

Part Three: Tickling the Funny Bone

Part Four: Creative Parenting

PART FIVE: THE THREE R's—RULES, REGULATIONS, AND RESPONSIBILITIES

Part Six: Rocky Roads—Troubles along the Way

Part Seven: The Soul in Parenting

PART EIGHT: PARENTS NEED CARE, TOO

EPILOGUE: YOUR MIRACULOUS FAMILY

SPECIAL THANKS

I would like to acknowledge the assistance, support, help, and wisdom of several people who participated with me in the birthing of this book. Their efforts and patience meant a great deal to me because I am a surgeon and a multiple personality who is not always easy to work with or understand. They are my agent, Andrea Hurst, and her assistants, Christina Lutman and Liz Barrett. I also want to extend heartfelt thanks and gratitude to the folks at Rodale for their assistance and the wonderful work they do, and a special thanks to Mariska van Aalst for her editing and guidance. The word *guidance* says it all: God—U and I—dancing the dance of creation. Bless you all.

*We are required to obtain a license to fish, hunt, or drive,
to practice medicine or law, or to open a business. However, we are not
required to be licensed prior to becoming a parent. I believe this book
can help you qualify for that license.*

—Bernie S. Siegel, MD

INTRODUCTION

The children of the future do not "belong" to their parents alone: They are the concern of every one of us; they are literally the hope of the world.

—Karl Menninger, MD

• • • •

The title of this book says it all. Love is necessary for our survival and is the key ingredient for both the parent and the child. Children see the magic in everything, and loving parents can and will experience so many magical moments while raising their children. Mudpies can be fun at times and also leave us covered with dirt.

When you look at your children and yourself, I'd like you to accept that you are all part of this special magical relationship. While creating your family, I'd like you to be in awe of life and its wonder but not hesitate to dive into life and take the risk of a mud bath now and then, too.

In my first book, *Love, Medicine & Miracles,* I share the stories of true survivors who refer to their diseases as blessings because of what being ill taught them about life. They taught me that beating a disease is not about being immortal but about how one lives in the face of adversity. They are the true heroes we can all learn from.

Love, Magic & Mudpies was written with the same goal in mind—I want to help parents not only survive the ups and downs of parenting but help them make it a blessing, too. The magic excites and enlightens us, while the mud can become the fertilizer for our lives and relationships. In this book, I will share with you the gems I have garnered from my medical practice and family life. From my experience as a father of five, grandfather of eight, pediatric surgeon, counselor to those with life-threatening illnesses, and a Chosen Dad for the suicidal and abused children I have met, I know our childhoods have a profound effect on our lifelong health. I've seen that what we learn in our earliest years has a direct effect on our self-esteem, behavior, and choices. It makes me realize that the parenting we receive is truly the number one health issue in most people's lives.

If you are reading this book, you probably already know that how we do or do not nurture our children will create their perception of the world. If children are to thrive, they must feel loved. If they do not, they literally have their growth stunted; all of their internal energy goes into protecting themselves and their survival. With healthy parenting and lots of love, our children have a better chance of growing up to be well-rounded human beings who accept themselves and who don't need to be destructive in order to get attention. The family becomes a community that works for the health and growth of everyone, not just one individual, just as the cells in the body work together for health and survival. To love is to enhance growth. Our beliefs are our biology, and our feelings reflect our internal chemistry. This is proven science.

Our children face many obstacles as they enter and swim through the sea of life. We need to be there when our kids get in over their heads, so we can pull them back to solid ground—or keep them on shore when the sea is turbulent. Our children need to know that when they are threatened by an unusually severe storm, they can turn to us to find a safe harbor. This book and its practical advice will enable you to watch over your children and teach you how to become their life preservers.

Parents face many new and diverse challenges in today's fast-paced world. From working around the clock for no monetary rewards to often getting little recognition for work well done, being a good parent is one of the most difficult jobs there is. What we need to remember is that we all have the potential to be great parents who produce superstars—however we choose to define that label. If we believe in our kids, consciously choose to nurture them, and make them believe in themselves, there are no limits to what can happen. This is not about imposing our desires upon our children or taking away their dreams and lives so we can be proud of them; it is about letting them know there are no limits to what they can achieve for themselves.

In this book, I will explore every aspect and stage of parenting, offering help to new parents, those with young children or teens, and parents facing an empty nest. If you have the desire and intention, this book will uplift, strengthen, and guide you through the inevitable ups, downs, joys, and heartaches of parenting; it may even help you rebirth and re-parent yourself. Remember, parents are the co-creators of life; so decide what you desire to create, and begin now. Your children are the finest raw material you will ever have to work with.

> *To believe in a child is to believe in the future. Through their aspirations they will save the world. With their combined knowledge the turbulent seas of hate and injustice will be calmed. They will champion the causes of life's underdogs, forging a society without class discrimination. They will supply humanity with music and beauty as it has never known. They will endure. Towards these ends I pledge my life's work. I will supply the children with tools and knowledge to overcome the obstacles. I will pass on the wisdom of my years and temper it with patience. I shall impact in each child the desire to fulfill his or her dream.*
>
> —HENRY JAMES

PART ONE

. . . .

ALL IN THE FAMILY— FAMILY LIFE AND VALUES

As a surgeon, I discovered very early on that we are all the same color inside. For me, our differences are not there to create separation or discrimination but to help us recognize the individuals who are members of our immediate family sitting with us at the dinner table.

Are you ready to love your children unconditionally, free of judgment and fear of the future? Sometimes our greatest fears and biggest problems become our teachers and blessings. When our children were born, I was very concerned about their physical wellness. When I watched our grandchildren being born, I was concerned about my ability to love them no matter what their bodies were like. I have matured. I am more open to accepting members into my family who may not be considered perfect, normal, or what I desired.

I have learned a great deal about love and family from children with various congenital anomalies, genetic problems, and Down syndrome. They have taught me more about completeness and love than any group I know. I can't help but share how one child with Down syndrome charged the hospital staff money every time they wanted to check his incision. I told him his surgeon shouldn't have to pay, and he allowed me free access to his wound. Another young man defined those who were mentally challenged as the people he "couldn't help get their love flow going."

No matter what your family does—whether your children, parents, in-laws, spouse, or relatives have disabilities, choose to practice a different religion, do poorly in school, become atheists, marry someone of another race, end up in jail instead of school, move across the country so you can't see your grandchildren, or just drive you nuts from Day One—they are still family and deserve to be loved, welcomed into your home, and nourished by your relationship.

What we share, which is more significant than our genes, is our love. What turns genes "on" and "off" is the environment they live in. Love is what every child needs, and love is what family is about. Sharing the birth of a child, a graduation, or a wedding unites us just as our losses bring us together. When we help our children and ourselves to grieve and survive our defects, losses, or mistakes without judgment or criticism, we are truly a loving family and will create survivors and thrivers.

An excellent role model would be the father of the boy in the story "The Emperor's New Clothes." Here is a child who sees what no one else is willing to see and who speaks what no one else has the courage to say publicly: The emperor has no clothes on. Does his father shush him, take him away, spank him, or put his hand over his mouth? No, he supports his child and acknowledges to everyone that his son is right. Think about how that child will feel growing up, knowing he has the support of his parents, and how proud you would feel being his parent. That support gives a child the freedom to be unique and authentic and frees him or her from the most common fear people have: "What do other people think of me?"

For me, family can be defined very simply: They are the people you would want at your bedside the day you were born and the ones you'd want there the day you die. Be the parent you would want your child to have. If you're not quite there yet, rehearse being that parent until you can become the parent your child needs and deserves. Accept your infant as a gift, and be prepared to live and learn. With love, children will thrive and teach you about life.

I keep thinking of how mother cats have been known to go into burning buildings to rescue their kittens. They don't ask questions about their offspring's value. They act out of love. Those who truly parent us provide us with the necessities of life: faith, hope, and love. They know that burning buildings come in many shapes and sizes.

BE THERE

An aware parent loves all children he or she meets and interacts with—for you are a caretaker for those moments in time.

—Doc Childre

. . . .

From the moment your child comes into this world, you need to be there for him or her. Even if you already have children, it is still not too late to *be there* because every moment you spend with your child counts. When we connect with another living thing, be it watching a birth or petting an animal, our entire body chemistry is changed. We continue to bond with other living things more easily after just one such experience.

Think of every moment you spend with your children or the children of others as part of this process. Each time you see a child, help him to come into the world in a way that makes him feel desired and loved. The newborn child especially depends on us to be there to protect, feed, and touch her as expressions of our love.

If no one is there for a newborn child, he or she cannot survive. I am not talking about simply feeding an infant; I am talking about being there physically, emotionally, and spiritually. In the finest orphanages in the 1800s, the mortality rate was well over 90 percent. Why? Because those caring for the infants thought they were spreading infections from one child to another, and so they stopped touching the children unless it was absolutely necessary. These children wasted away and died. Those who were fortunate enough to be held or touched while the maintenance people performed their tasks were the ones who survived.

So be there for your children, and touch their bodies and lives in every way you can. You may not do it right every time, but as long as they know you care, it will make a difference. They will know your hands are available to catch them whenever they fall. The opposite of love is indifference, and indifference can harden even the strongest heart.

HOW TO MAKE THE MAGIC: Spending time with your children and giving them emotional support are the most important things you can do for them. So take time out of every day and ask them about what is going on in their lives and if there is anything you can help them with. Ask how you can be there for them in some way, be it physically, emotionally, spiritually, or even financially. If you do this often, they will know that you will always have the time to be there for them.

PAY THE BILLS,
BUT HAVE SOME FUN

*The easiest way for your children to learn about money is for you
not to have any.*

—KATHARINE WHITEHORN

• • • •

amilies are expensive from Day One. The US Department of Agriculture estimates that it costs more than $280,000 to raise a child from birth through age 17—and that does not include the cost of any private schools (including preschool), expensive medical bills, ballet lessons, braces, high-end sneakers, cars, or anything else that parents might consider a luxury but kids see as a necessity. Nor does it include the single biggest expense parents will ever pay: supporting kids through college, which typically ranges from $20,000 to $150,000.

You can imagine my horror when I visualized the rude economics of having had five children within seven years. It looked like sheer financial disaster to me. First it would apparently cost me a couple of million to get them through high school (if we stuck to a budget), then they would all be in college or graduate school—at the same time. I didn't see any way I could ever afford it. The future looked bleak. But I was able to stop and recognize that I was acting like some of my patients who'd been diagnosed with life-threatening diseases: They couldn't enjoy the life they were living because they were focused only on the disastrous future they imagined.

As a doctor, I had seen and learned through experience that the future unfolds as it is meant to, not necessarily as we fear it might or as statistics suggest it will. I gave up worrying about money, and we raised our children with faith, hope, and love instead. We weren't always able to buy them everything that they wanted, but we learned together to be practical and to ask for help when we needed it. And we learned to have fun along the way.

American author Ernestine Ulmer wrote, "Life is uncertain. Eat dessert first." Don't deny yourself vacations or little treats or any other moments of joy unless you can do it completely out of love and truly feel good about it. I buy lottery tickets when I have a couple of extra dollars. After all, somebody has to win. Why not me? It's fun to open the newspaper and check the numbers. So far I haven't hit it big, but I've had a lot of fun playing. I don't waste my time wishing and praying to win the lottery because I know that what I truly need isn't dollars, but peace of mind. I need the ability to be grateful that I can pay my bills much more than I need a quick fix to get rid of them.

Life always presents us with solutions if we are willing to take notice. You may need to take two jobs to help your kids, or they may win scholarships, or they may decide to delay attending college or enter a trade school. Life has a way of working out while we are living in a solution rather than dwelling on a problem. And whenever you find yourself in doubt, just repeat this phrase: "Thank you for everything. I have no complaint whatsoever."

HOW TO MAKE THE MAGIC: Teach your children to prepare for the future, but not at the expense of enjoying the present. Give them piggy banks as soon as they are old enough to understand anything about money. Each week, hand them a dollar in quarters. Tell them they must put three in the bank, and they can spend one on whatever they want. When they are older, you can give them more than a dollar, as long as you break the money down into smaller denominations so they can immediately put most of it in the bank and keep a little for pocket money. The ability to save will give them peace of mind later; the pocket money will help them taste the "dessert" first!

PLAN THEIR BIRTH ORDER (AND SEX)

Before I was married I had six theories about raising children.
Now I have six children and no theories.

—JOHN WILMOT

. . . .

Okay, so you might not be able to plan your children's birth order. And as far as I know, you can't really plan their sex either. But know that the birth sequence plays an undeniable role in what each child is like from the standpoint of intellect, interests, future professions, social expertise, and more. A firstborn or only child is more likely to become a professional and not be as social as the seventh child, who from Day One has to learn to deal with noise, people, competition, and parents who are too busy to worry about what does or does not interest him or her.

Studies reveal how birth order affects the personality of the child and even what profession he or she is likely to choose. After all, the firstborn has two adults to communicate with, then later a sibling. Child number one is more likely to be the professional and not as comfortable with people as child number five, who is surrounded by people and spends far less time with his adult parents.

And while you can't do much to make it happen, it can also make a difference to have an oldest daughter, even more than one daughter, so they can talk to each other. Your family will then be blessed with more than one mother figure. In each generation of our family, we keep ending up with one girl. Poor thing has no one to talk to because boys are just different that way. Our daughter had to become good at screaming and running from her brothers as a survival behavior to get her parents' attention so they could rescue her. (Nothing like finding a curled-up snake when you uncover your typewriter.)

When he was a teenager, our oldest son asked me about his younger siblings: "How come they don't have to do what I had to do when I was growing up?" I told him it was because I had learned that many things I had asked him to do were not very important. Apparently, he was glad I was becoming enlightened, so he let me go.

I may add that this was not just about how they kept their room and other such day-to-day issues. This realization was also about things that initially didn't make sense to me, like the question of whether or not to go to school and focus on an education without taking time off to pursue other interests. But when the third, fourth, or fifth child wants to do something different, even contrary to everything you believe to be "right," you end up finding yourself saying the unthinkable: "Sure, go ahead, if that's what you want."

> **HOW TO MAKE THE MAGIC:** Notice how birth order plays out in your family. Are you different in how you parent child number one than child number two, three, and so on? Of course, loving your children, no matter what their order, is the most important thing of all. You'll probably see that the oldest is more likely to be intellectual and a loner, while the youngest in a large family is more likely to get along better with people and tolerate noise. And if your kids can accept certain aspects of themselves and their personalities as related to their birth order, they'll likely be less critical of themselves.

SIBLING RIVALRY

With one child, you become a parent; with two,
you are promoted to a referee.

—Unknown

• • • •

When children are born into a large family, there is often sibling rivalry. Because the children are competing with their brothers and sisters for the parents' attention, this rivalry truly can teach survival behavior. They learn to express themselves, make noise, and be heard so they are not treated with less respect than their siblings. They learn to speak up so they can have new clothes, too, and not have to wear only what their older brothers or sisters outgrow.

They learn that they can form teams and overcome individual siblings who create problems or bully them. So sibling rivalry is not all bad. It does, however, take its toll on the furniture, fixtures, doors, and walls—but that is all part of growing up. Our children's bedroom doors all had holes in them from the frequent battering they underwent. When we were preparing to sell our first house to move to a bigger one, the kids came to me and mentioned the various holes and marks visible to prospective purchasers. They felt embarrassed and wanted me to repair the damage. I refused and told them I would explain to everyone how it occurred and that if they bought the house, I would pay for the repairs. It helped me get even and made them think about what they were doing.

Life is about competition and rivalry. What better place to be trained than the family, where love is present? Children can act out and still be welcomed back into the house. The competition of sibling rivalry is not about making their brothers and sisters look bad; it is about creating their individuality. Every child should have the feeling that he or she can do it better than older siblings and give it a shot. Every single child is unique and special in his or her own way. So let them know that they have their own talents to give the world.

One of our sons took dancing classes, and we had no problem with our son the dancer. It was his thing. Others played the drums, restored cars, raised pets and farm animals, painted pictures, and did their things. I found that each of them opened up new vistas for me and helped me learn and develop new interests. The problem is that our house is filled to the rafters with their things. Lord knows I feel very attached to my kids, but they do not feel the need to take all the items to their homes now that they have their own lives to lead. So their closets and rooms look like they did when they left home years ago.

Hey, it just occurred to me for the first time: They are getting even for my embarrassing them years ago!

HOW TO MAKE THE MAGIC: Let your children know that although they are different, it is these differences that make them unique and beautiful. Take the time to share each one's interest as an individual and as a family. When our children were young, we would all go roller-skating on Thursday nights; but individually as parents, we took the time to enjoy our children's dance classes, band performances, cars, or pet shows. Let your children know that competition is fine, but so is teaching and sharing interests with each other. When they realize they don't have to be rivals for their parents' love, their differences become gifts and not problems. Help them to find and develop their own talents. (When our children wanted my assistance, one condition I made was for them to become truly educated about their interests. This has benefited them for a lifetime and opened up my world, too.) Also try to find a way to give each of them an area in the house that is their territory to study and sleep in; call it their sanctuary. This is a place where they can feel safe to explore their interests and not worry about how it looks to others.

MOTTOES TO LIVE
OR DIE BY

*If there is anything that we wish to change in the child,
we should first examine it and see whether it is not something
that could better be changed in ourselves.*

—C. G. JUNG

• • • •

One of the most heartbreaking experiences I have had—over and over again—is listening to people with life-threatening illnesses as they discuss their childhoods. It breaks my heart because so many of them did not grow up with devoted parents like mine. I always felt loved as a child, even when my parents did not like something I had said or done. They believed in me and trusted me to live up to my word, just as I trusted them to live up to theirs. There were times when, far from home, I would refuse to join my friends in some risky activity because I had told my parents I wouldn't do it. My friends were dumbfounded, because my parents obviously would have had no way of knowing what I did when they weren't there. But they were always with me in spirit, so I kept my word.

My parents instilled those values in me. They gave me mottoes to live by. "Do what will make you happy," they told me. "Problems are God's redirections, and something good will come of them," they assured. Many years later, I offered workshops for people facing terminal illness. I asked them what mottoes they were living by. I once was interrupted by a participant who wanted to know: "You're not asking us about what mottoes we are dying by?" That person, like too many others, grew up with verbally abusive parents who repeated negative and hurtful mottoes all day long: "You were not wanted." "You will always be a failure at whatever you try." "We'll never be proud of you." "There's something wrong with you."

One woman said, "My mother's words were always eating away at me. I think maybe they were what caused my cancer." She, and many others in my workshops, had no problem writing homework assignments about why they should commit suicide, yet they had a lot of trouble writing about why they were worth living and loving. I try to help people like that by showing them how to re-parent themselves. In some cases I become a CD (Chosen Dad). By loving them, I may help them come to love themselves and let go of their painful pasts. Then they can finally begin to live as the divine children they truly are.

HOW TO MAKE THE MAGIC: Think of a life-enhancing statement you can say to yourself today. Practice saying it to a photograph of yourself until you truly mean it. When you are ready, share it with your children. Know that these are the words that will echo in their heads for years to come.

DON'T BE AFRAID TO FAIL

I have not failed. I've just found 10,000 ways that won't work.

—Thomas Alva Edison

. . . .

As parents, we often feel like we fall short or fail to be the best parents we can be. The same is true when your kids fail at something in their first attempts. *Failure* is a word that has as many meanings as there are people who experience it. It can be a disaster or an opportunity.

A young man once went to a rich, well-known business executive and told him how much he wanted to succeed, yet had failed thus far. The executive told the young man that he simply had not failed enough yet. He needed to take more risks and find out what wouldn't work in order to develop a keen intuition about strategies and tactics that would succeed.

Always teach your kids to remember that there is a huge difference between experiencing a setback or disappointment and being a failure as a person. When you feel you are a failure, life becomes a bitter and painful experience. This advice holds true not just for business and finance but for career choices, relationships, and all other aspects of life as well.

Consider this true story: When President Jimmy Carter had to comment to the press on the disastrous results of the US military's attempt to rescue American hostages from Iran in 1980, he refused to accept defeat, describing the fiasco not as a failure but as "an incomplete success." He was harshly ridiculed by the public and the press, but he did not give in to the idea that he was a failure. Instead, he persevered in his attempts to secure the release of the hostages via negotiations. He lost his bid for reelection that year, but he succeeded in getting all 52 of the hostages released—on the very day he left office. He went on to be awarded the Nobel Peace Prize in 2002 "for his decades of untiring effort to find peaceful solutions to international conflicts."

Help your kids to learn that if they are afraid to risk being an "incomplete success," they will never achieve their goals. A line that really helps me comes from the movie *Harold and Maude*, in which Ruth Gordon played an 80-year-old woman trying to help a bored, frightened, and confused young man. She smiled broadly and shouted like a cheerleader: "Give me an L! Give me an I! Give me a V! Give me an E! L-I-V-E! Live!" Then she added the kicker, in a softer voice: "Otherwise you've got nothing to talk about in the locker room."

A good failure can actually be kind of funny when you can detach from it a bit and find the humor in your mistakes or in the chain of circumstances that led to the pratfall. Give your kids, and yourself, permission to L-I-V-E live. As Ruth Gordon also said in the movie: "Reach out. Take a chance. Get hurt even. Play as well as you can. Go, team, go."

> **HOW TO MAKE THE MAGIC:** Teach yourself and your family that you have nothing to lose and a lot to learn. Talk to your children when they feel they have made mistakes or failed and help them to see what they learned from their experiences. Make sure they know that even if something did not turn out as planned, they are not failures.

FAMILY VACATIONS

Your children need your presence more than they need your presents.

—Jesse Jackson

. . . .

Finding a place where all seven of us would be happy on our vacation was sometimes quite a chore. To get some ideas, I would look in magazines and ask friends about places that they had visited. One place we enjoyed was Colonel Skillen's Farm in Maine. We drove up there several summers and stayed together in a cabin on the farm. The Colonel was a retired army officer, and he and his wife prepared meals for everyone who stayed with them. They had farm animals and many horses, so the entire family could go out riding. When our children were younger, they would just sit on the horses' backs for a slow walk around the farm. The cold ocean and nearby lake provided a wonderful place for the kids to have active, outdoor fun.

At the other extreme, we also loved going to New York City, sharing a hotel room for the weekend and visiting the many museums, the planetarium, art galleries, Central Park, and, of course, the major toy stores. When they were older and I was invited to Hawaii,

I made sure we all went together. The photographs of that time together still make me a happy parent.

Ultimately, after adding up the cost of sending the children to camp and the vacations, I realized that it was cheaper to buy and own a vacation house we could go to whenever we wanted. Since our honeymoon had been on Cape Cod, we migrated back there with the kids. We found a little house and made it our own, spending a good portion of the year there for vacations and weekend getaways. We could bring all the pets and kids in the Suburban and just feel right at home. I named the house Seagull's Folly after the purchase of Alaska, which was called Seward's Folly because people thought a lot of money was spent on land worth very little. I had the same experience. But to me, it was and is now worth every penny.

Even with our four-wheel drive, I got stuck in the sand until I learned how to deflate the tires for better traction. But it was great to just ride out on the beach and spend time as a family fishing, surfing, sunbathing, and playing in the sand. That house has so many memories in it that it is therapeutic just to walk in. We all became younger there.

Family vacations are key to reenergizing the relationships within your family. Taking this time to be together without the obligations of the outside world shows how strong your bonds are and how special these moments can be. You don't need a vacation home to find your therapeutic space. Just find somewhere to go or something to do that everyone enjoys and have fun!

HOW TO MAKE THE MAGIC: Surprise everyone with a special vacation that you have planned. It can be to a local bed-and-breakfast or to a distant Pacific island. The place and the cost are not important. Just get everyone together and create a time when you can be a family. Enjoy these moments, mishaps and all, and your legacy of fun will create great stories to share that will bring a smile to everyone's face at family get-togethers.

FAMILY THERAPY

Like all parents, my husband and I just do the best we can, hold our breath,
and hope we've set aside enough money to pay for our kids' therapy.

—MICHELLE PFEIFFER

. . . .

Everybody has heard of group therapy, but how many know about GrouPet therapy? I created it for animal lovers of all ages. You sit down with the animals of your choice for two hours every week and work out your problems with their help. For instance, I meet with four cats that nap through most of the session, so I get to improve my public speaking abilities. I rely on bunnies when I need a soft tummy to rub. Lions teach me to control my words and emotions so I don't make them angry, and I have learned to schedule our meetings for after they had a good meal. Dolphins are great about intuitively knowing my needs and giving me some fun time in the pool. The idea is to learn from your experience with your pets about how to enhance your personality and behavior. It works because everyone looks forward to weekly sessions when their pets are involved, when they can feel free of stress and judgment, and when their family is not part of the group.

My latest venture into counseling is FFFT: Fun For Family Therapy. I know from personal and unpleasant experience that fun is sorely needed and seldom allowed in therapy. Our family dragged itself to more dreadful sessions than I care to remember. Each of those sessions was notable, not for the growth we experienced, but for the therapist's interminable focus on all our problems. I always tried to lighten things up, but my efforts were rarely appreciated (except by our kids, who missed my presence when a medical emergency kept me from attending). That's why I came up with FFFT; it will be something the family looks forward to simply because it will be fun for everyone.

Here's how it will work. Every week the family will get together for a "therapy" session, the entire point of which is to come up with something really fun that the whole family will enjoy doing together. It can be something as simple as going to a funny movie or as complex as building a snowman that's an exact replica of a family member. The therapy works best when families include as possible activities the many strange or exotic interests of family members. Our family has gone to rock concerts to hear one of our sons play the drums with his band and to herpetology society meetings (and distant exotic pet stores) to admire reptiles that another one of our kids collected. We also like to travel together. In some places, kids are able to see how fortunate they are to enjoy such a high standard of living at home, while in others (the Hawaiian Islands, for example), the entire family can indulge in fantasies of living happily ever after in paradise.

To make it official, you could always invite a licensed therapist to come along. Then that person could see what a healthy, happy family actually looks like.

HOW TO MAKE THE MAGIC: Ask each member of the family to write down two activities the family would enjoy doing together. One of the activities should involve no more than a day or an evening, while the other might take longer, maybe a week or two, including travel. No one should sign their list; just fold the paper in half and drop it in a shoe box. If you have a small family, have everyone fill out two. Then read aloud each list and vote for the best suggestions. Take the two favorite ideas and start making plans. Save the rest of the list for the future.

DEFINE SUCCESS

Success is not the key to happiness. Happiness is the key to success.

—A<small>LBERT</small> S<small>CHWEITZER</small>

• • • •

What is your definition of success, and how do you pass it on to your children? In a materialistic society such as ours, it can sometimes be difficult to live by a personal definition of success that is based on generosity, honesty, and happiness rather than on the accumulation of wealth. Most role models for success that dominate newspapers, magazines, and television are rich, famous, incredibly good-looking people—who almost never work in professions that help others, like teaching or nursing or running charities. There is immense pressure on kids to succeed but little emphasis on how to define success for themselves.

One day a young man from a very wealthy family walked into my office. Besides his illness, his major complaint was that his father had ruined his life. I asked him what his father had done and he replied, "He gave me a million dollars when I was twenty-one." I remember thinking that there were many people in my waiting room that day who would have loved to relieve that young man of his "burden." So I asked him how receiving such a nice sum of money could have ruined his life. He answered: "I have to be a success."

Things were slightly different in our family. When my father died, he left each of his grandchildren sixty thousand dollars. (I wouldn't have worried so much about paying for their educations if I had known that was going to happen.) Yet when our son Keith enrolled in college, he called me and said he needed money to pay his tuition. Naturally, I reminded him that he had sixty thousand dollars to pay for his own education. He surprised me with his answer.

"I gave it to a friend I made when I visited Nepal," he said, "so he could come here to get an education and then return to help his people."

If you were Keith's parent, which boy would you be proud of—the one trying to be a success or the one who gave the money away? I wasn't feeling particularly enlightened that day because Keith's generosity meant that I had to come up with the money for his tuition. In time, however, I became impressed with what Keith had done. I thought back on the boy whose father burdened him with a million dollars. I wonder what would have happened if he had decided to use the money to start a charity for homeless pets or to dig wells in Africa for people who had no clean water. Would he have felt like a success? Would his father have yelled at him for wasting his money?

HOW TO MAKE THE MAGIC: Think of ways to demonstrate to your children that material things are to be used to make the world a better place to live. Ask them to go through the newspaper for at least a week and clip articles about people or animals who need help, such as victims of natural disasters, fire, or crime. Then sit down together and review those cases to see how your children might help, with time or with money or other donations. Maybe you'll raise a future head of the United Nations, Red Cross, or Humane Society.

IN-LAWS OR OUTLAWS

Be kind to your mother-in-law,
but pay for her board at some good hotel.

—JOSH BILLINGS

• • • •

It is hard enough to raise a child without the criticism of close family members. But before you take offense, please understand that feedback and constructive criticism can be useful and helpful. When I share with our now-grown children some of the problems we faced raising them, I can give them a few clues as to how to avoid the same missteps we made. Whether your challenge is being a parent, baking a cake, or tackling a physical disease, it is better to learn from the wisdom of those who have preceded you than from your own mistakes. I was fortunate to marry a schoolteacher who knew how to keep children active and safe. However, I didn't always have her around. But now I can confidently tell our kids that when they are imitating my parenting behavior by letting their kids swing from trees, they are risking injury to their children.

Whether it's from family or friends who share their experiences raising children, advice can polish the mirror of a new parent. But if you find you are repeatedly being told—by, say, your mother-in-law—what you are doing wrong, the results will likely be additional family relationship problems and additional stress. Watch out when Grandma starts constantly telling you what to do and how to do it—trouble's coming. Sure, when the kids are older and visiting Grandma, you can take a deep breath, relax, and let Grandma do her thing. But when you are back in your own territory, you are the one who decides the rules and regulations that govern your family and home.

When Grandma or another person comes over and starts in with often unwelcome advice and criticism, the best response is not to discuss who is right and why, but instead to smile and say, "Thank you very much. I love you. Perhaps you'd like the kids to come and stay with you." If you keep repeating that offer, I guarantee they will give up and stop driving you nuts. By generously proposing to have them take the children more than they really want to, you may find them becoming less and less outspoken.

> **HOW TO MAKE THE MAGIC:** Put pictures of the in-laws around the house and practice saying the sentence above to the pictures. That will make it easier to do when the real thing shows up. Also practice saying, "That's not what my mother or father said or did." This way the blame goes onto another generation, and they can work it out among themselves. The idea, and the desired outcome everyone wants, is to have their advice be helpful, not critical.

SPORTS AND KIDS

Our children are watching us live, and what we are shouts louder than anything we can say.

—HENRY DOHERTY

. . . .

When I was a counselor at a day camp, I always chose the clumsiest, least athletic boys to be on my team. Why? Because I knew how it felt to stand there waiting to be picked. Our team never won anything, but I had a lot of happy kids on it. I can remember chubby Stuart's parents telling me this was the first summer he seemed to be enjoying camp. I didn't tell them why.

Think of the good old days when games were played on the street or at nearby playgrounds with no leagues, schedules, or parents around. What a great life experience for the child—the structure was loose and the objective was to have fun. There was no pressure on the kids to perform; all they had to do was enjoy the sport that interested them.

In today's families, when the children participate in sports, it is all about schedules and competition. There are the soccer moms constantly chauffeuring their kids everywhere—

from practices to games. In the news, you read about fathers who beat up coaches and scream obscenities from the stands—a fine example to set for the kids. Winning becomes everything, and if you don't win, you're a loser, and no one is proud of a loser. In the book *Tuesdays with Morrie,* Morrie, a college professor, is sitting in the stands at a school basketball game while everyone shouts, "We're number one!" He gets up and goes down to the court and yells back, "What's wrong with being number two?"

That message really hit home for me while I was running my first New York Marathon. A woman on the sidewalk kept repeating, "You're all winners." And she was right. No matter when you finish, they hang a medal around your neck.

HOW TO MAKE THE MAGIC: Remember, for your family it isn't always about being first or how fast you get there—it is about enjoying and doing your best at what you set out to do. If your children are involved in sports, notice how the schedule is affecting the entire family. Is your child really enjoying the game? Does he or she feel pressured into performing? What values is your child learning from the coach, other players, family members, and peers? As Fred Engh, the president of the National Alliance for Youth Sports, said, "We have too many parents trying to live through their kids. They all think they're raising the next Michael Jordan." Consider your ultimate goal for your kid's athletic pursuits—is it fitness and fun, or fame and fortune? Adjust your attitude accordingly. Your kids will take all their cues from you.

HUDDLE UP

Television has made a semicircle out of the family circle.

—Author Unknown

• • • •

When I talk to parents, I often tell them to get the family or gang all together for at least a few minutes as part of their daily and weekly routine. This recommendation stems from a realization I had recently that few families ever set time aside to sit down and spend time together. Just as a football team gets into a huddle before each play to get their signals straight, the family also needs to huddle up on a regular basis. While gathered together, it is a great time to share goals, make plans, and prepare to take action, either individually or as a group.

Mealtimes used to center around sharing food with loved ones while sitting around a table. No longer. Little meaningful conversation happens during meals these days or during the normal, busy family routine—not to mention the sound of the TV blaring away at the same time the family is eating or trying to have any type of conversation. When families watch TV while doing any other activity, the circle is broken, and all the attention is on the TV screen and not on each other.

I suggest that every family set up a scheduled meeting time, so that everyone knows when the family huddle will be each week. Yes, there are legitimate excuses for missing the meeting, but it should be a high priority for every family member to attend. This insistence upon attendance is not about obsessive behavior; it's about placing a premium on sharing and communicating with each other and bringing everyone closer.

This meeting can take place when the family is out for dinner or during exercise, such as a walk or bike ride. The get-together is something you want people to look forward to and enjoy, so it should not become sermon time but a true time for sharing, listening, and learning. Make sure to include humor, too, and stories about the good things that have happened each week. Don't focus exclusively on what's wrong but on what's right and how you can have even more fun together.

HOW TO MAKE THE MAGIC: Let the family know that you would like to start a weekly meeting or huddle and are open to ideas on how to set up the format. Share your enthusiasm and excitement about these meetings with everyone, and get them on board. Be creative and flexible when scheduling your days and times. Presuming the weather will let you, one great idea is to take everyone to a scenic place and have a picnic. Then sit around on the blanket and talk about the future and the part everyone plays on the family team and how you can each score a touchdown. Never leave gratitude out of the huddle; keep it as the quarterback coordinating every play.

WHEN THEY DON'T COME ONE AT A TIME

If it's two more boys, I'm not coming home from the hospital.

—BARBARA SIEGEL

• • • •

Many years ago, I remember Elisabeth Kübler-Ross, renowned psychiatrist and author, discussing her experience as a triplet. Since each parent had only one lap to sit on, she felt neglected and unloved compared to her sisters. Later, my wife and I decided to have one more child. After delivering three sons, we wanted a daughter. This was during the years before the ultrasound was available, and two weeks before her due date she had an x-ray that revealed twins. (We had thought her big tummy was due to the stretch from previous pregnancies!)

Multiple births leave both you and your children with many issues to deal with, such as giving the children equal amounts of your time and love. I would advise you to ask for or hire the help you need to preserve your health and peace of mind. Trying to do everything and not giving yourself time to rest isn't fair to anyone.

Your children want and need your attention, but there is a limit to what one person can provide. We had assistance from our family, lots of neighborhood teenagers, my patients, and our friends as babysitters and pseudo parents. We also took some time for ourselves, once the children were old enough, to get away for a weekend. This was therapeutic for the kids, too, because they were able to have a vacation from our stress!

I would also advise giving children who are the result of a multiple birth specific chores to do so they can become an effective team, rotating their chores so they do not develop limited abilities and do not rely on each other too heavily. This will help them to become more independent and able to handle various situations on their own.

From the children's perspective, it is essential that they feel loved and that their parents give them the time they deserve. When you can't be there physically, your words can be with them. Tell them you love them and that the only reason you are not there all the time is that you have other obligations in your life. Let them know they are always important to you, even when you are not there.

How to Make the Magic: Whether it is handing out chores or giving presents, make a conscious effort to be fair and equal with all your children. When children are not encouraged or are not given as much responsibility or praise, they feel as though they are being ignored or neglected. Many children act out and cause trouble for this very reason. It is their way of saying "Pay attention to me!" So stay in tune with how much you are singling out one child for attention or punishment. Your family will be happier and healthier when everyone feels equally special and loved.

USING FEEDBACK FROM SCHOOLTEACHERS

Teaching is not just a job. It is a human service,
and it must be thought of as a mission.

—Dr. Ralph Tyler

. . . .

"Mom, the teacher called me a scurvy elephant today in class." I can remember receiving this quote from a cancer patient who said her son came home from school and told her what the teacher said. I advise my patients not to be submissive but to speak up and be responsible participants and characters when they are hospitalized. This mom had taken my philosophy to heart as a parent, too. The next day she went to school with her son and asked the teacher why she had called her son a scurvy elephant. Her son's teacher laughed and said, "Your son is a bright kid, but he keeps speaking out and interrupting the class. I told him he was a 'disturbing element.'"

Teachers play an important part in family life. Another woman I know has cancer and is facing a truly life-threatening situation. She is worrying more about her children and how they are handling her illness and what will happen to them if she dies. Her sons' teachers have told her how well they are doing in school and that they seem to be adjusting to the mother's illness far better than she thinks.

Teachers who have gotten to know your children, whether in front of a blackboard or behind a piano, are reliable judges when stressful family situations are occurring. Do not hesitate to, and in fact be sure you do, inform your children's teachers and the school nurse when a problem arises in the family. Whether you write a letter or go in and talk is up to you, but make sure the lines of communication are kept open. This will help the teacher to understand the reasons behind a child's unusual behavior and address it accordingly.

Feedback from a teacher is not to be feared. When a teacher tells you there is a problem, you can use this feedback to guide you to the proper therapeutic resource. Learn to listen to your children and those who care for, coach, and teach them. Their feedback will help you to better know the needs of your child and will give you guidance and direction about how to address them.

> **HOW TO MAKE THE MAGIC:** Send a questionnaire to your children's teachers and ask them for honest feedback about you and your children. You can start by asking if they have any comments to make about how your child is doing in school and behaving in class. Then you can ask specific questions about how he or she gets along with classmates, in sports or group activities, with the opposite sex, or with any specific problem that concerns you. Do not be afraid of the answers. If they know you care, they will respect you and the job you are doing as a parent. Remember, as with parents and in-laws: Criticism can polish your mirror.

HIDDEN TALENTS

I believe that every person is born with talent.

—Maya Angelou

. . . .

Every child is like a seed—hidden within each is a unique talent. The other day, I watched a three-year-old playing a violin with a concert orchestra. He had apparently picked up the instrument when he was two and started playing.

That experience made me remember the time when my parents arranged for me to have piano lessons. I would make my fingers sticky so the keys would adhere to them and the teacher would have trouble instructing me. After a few weeks of this, she explained to my mother that the piano was not my thing. I did turn out to have visual talents, became an artist as a child, and enjoyed attending art classes. My parents took me to classes where I had a chance to create art and develop that talent instead of insisting that I sit at the piano while it took me more than thirty years just to learn to sing on key. What was interesting to me was that I was aware of my talent but had no concept of the art world, or I might have chosen it as a career. So let your children follow their hearts and gifts. If they can earn a living doing what they love, they will never have to spend any time "working."

Our talents are diverse for many reasons. I believe everything plays a part, from past lives to how our brains are wired due to inherited genetic traits and talents. No matter what the etiology is, the important thing is to give your child the freedom to explore his or her talents and skills and not to direct your child only to what you may find interesting. What is likely to impress the neighbors or a college admissions committee is not going to help your child to grow or find his or her individual path.

Help your children follow their feelings and explore their unique talents and interests by taking them to exhibits, museums, and shows of all sorts. Bring home musical instruments, art supplies, a variety of sports equipment, chemistry sets, and games involving knowledge, skills, and abilities. Our home is still filled with interesting boxes that I keep trying to donate to various organizations. Remember, this may have nothing to do with your children's future careers, but when they discover their passions or abilities, they might find the path they want to follow. Expose them to the world of creativity and let them go their way. Discovering your talent too late in life, or only after you find that your lifetime is limited, can be tragic.

HOW TO MAKE THE MAGIC: Arrange to take your children to concerts, museums, and exhibitions of all sorts, as well as to practical places where they can see people doing things from repairing automobiles to welding metal into works of art. The world is a place full of diversity and beauty, so help them to find their unique talents through role models and examples that they would never have discovered on their own.

SCHOOL DAYS

She started school this morning,
And she seemed so very small.
As I walked there beside her
In the Kindergarten hall . . .
And I must share my little girl
With friends and work and play;
She's not a baby anymore—
She's in Kindergarten today.

—FIRST DAY OF KINDERGARTEN SCHOOL POEM, AUTHOR UNKNOWN

• • • •

Adrienne Coleman has been a kindergarten teacher in our area for almost twenty years. She says, "Kindergarten is a year when children need space and parents are at a loss at how to manage, a year where children need boundaries, eye contact, and a predictable day. It's a confusing time for parents and a high-impact year for kids."

In talking to her, and recalling my wife's experience as a kindergarten teacher and mine as a pediatric surgeon, I can agree with her. When children start school, their brain wave patterns reveal that they are reaching a point where they can begin to deal with their own consciousness and become less vulnerable to subliminal messages from their parents. Geneticist Bruce Lipton discusses many of these factors in his work and book *Biology of Belief.* Basically, at age six, children begin to become conscious of what is transpiring around them and realize they can react to it and disagree rather than become indoctrinated to the message imposed upon them. To quote our grandson Jarrod around age five, "You aren't parents. You are monsters. You don't treat me like a child. You treat me like nothing." We didn't have to worry about him being under anyone's spell. He is a sweetheart now and very much his own person.

Parents of kindergarteners need to remind themselves not to focus only on what their children's grades will be and what they'll be proud of. They need to let their kids make mistakes without being embarrassed so they can learn from them. Children of all ages need to have their secrets, too. Parents don't need to know what they did every minute of every day. Children need room and space and time to become who they are and want to be.

I once met parents whose child had died, and they were mad at God for taking their brilliant son, who got excellent grades at school. The mother pulled his test papers out of her pocketbook to show me. All I could think of was that if I had died before my mom, I hope she would have something other than my test papers as her most significant memory of me.

Let your children grow and become conscious in their own ways. Give them room and space to enjoy themselves and their activities. In kindergarten they are still young and free and need time to play and rest. You don't have to insist they participate in all the things you wish you had done or think they need to do to keep up with other families. Enjoy your children while they are young and while they still want to spend time with you!

HOW TO MAKE THE MAGIC: Consider each of your children to be a seed. Bring them together and ask what kind of seed they would like to be. Their choices will help you to know them better. An acorn will not enjoy being a daffodil just because that is what you want in your front yard.

LET 'EM GROW UP

You have to do your own growing no matter how tall
your grandfather was.

—Abraham Lincoln

• • • •

I am always thinking about the struggles children go through as they find their way down the road of life. One song I know talks about these years in terms of curves, hills, and tunnels we must confront along the way. These challenges are especially tough for children because they are just learning how to "drive" through life.

Think back to when you first learned to drive a car. Remember all the time and effort that went into making sure you would learn how to do it safely? Well, there are no seat belts to keep you safe on this drive.

The most fundamental part of our job as parents is to keep our kids safe, but being safe isn't all there is to life. We have to ask ourselves how we want them to experience life. Do we want them to grow up knowing how to face the world? Or do we want to keep them hidden from the world and not let them grow up? The preferred answers to these questions may seem obvious. Of course we want them to grow up. But deep inside, we might be more fearful and overprotective than we realize.

It's tough for kids to grow up and be independent, but it's even tougher to be denied that opportunity. I see this very clearly in my teen patients with life-threatening illnesses. They can't grow up and move out into the world on their own. Illness forces them to become children again as their lives are limited by their treatment and disease. They can easily become very depressed on top of being physically ill.

We parents need to be able to step back and let our kids grow up, no matter what they are facing. We need to empower them to make their own decisions. It is their life and, as difficult as it may be, we need to let them live it. Even if it seems scary to us, we have to let go and give them the freedom they need to grow up.

HOW TO MAKE THE MAGIC: Make a list of decisions and lifestyles you have imposed upon your children, from health to hairstyles. Then sit down with them and talk about it. Ask them how they felt about those decisions and lifestyle "choices." Make sure the conversation is age appropriate, but don't be afraid to reach out and let them surprise you with their wisdom. When your kids participate in choices for their lives, they will not have to step over boundary lines to get your attention because they have freely chosen those lines for themselves.

PART TWO

LOVE IS THE MAIN INGREDIENT

Several years ago, at the conclusion of writing my book *Prescriptions for Living*, I wrote a recipe for what I called life pudding. The key ingredient for my pudding is love. You cannot consume too much love nor become deficient by giving too much away. Nothing makes your life feel as full as love. Love benefits both the giver and the receiver and is absolutely necessary for the survival of our species. So the more you serve and share love, the better everyone feels.

What problem can you think of that love cannot help someone live through? I know a minister who, while being robbed, said to the man robbing her, "I know behind that mask is someone I could love." He dropped her purse, left her house, and returned years later to thank her.

We all need loving parents. Who they are isn't the issue. A loving parent can be a neighbor, grandparent, teacher, or minister who, through his or her love, makes you feel like a beloved child. The most important ingredient you can bring to your family, your life, and the world is love.

LOVE AT FIRST SIGHT

This was love at first sight, love everlasting: a feeling unknown, unhoped for, unexpected—insofar as it could be a matter of conscious awareness; it took entire possession of him, and he understood, with joyous amazement, that this was for life.

—Thomas Mann

. . . .

You cannot help but love your children the first time you see them. When my wife was pregnant, I would watch her body change as she created new life. I remember the excitement and thrill of feeling the infant move within her. When you watch a child being born or see the baby for the first time, you are changed by the experience. The love hormones within you surge, especially with your own child. You are altered, physically and emotionally, and so become one with the magic of creation.

I can recall bringing home one of our newborn children and watching his siblings lay eyes on him for the first time. Their expressions were just as beautiful as the baby, because they were in awe of this beautiful infant and a new life. I think it also helped them to feel more angelic and divine because they realized we were all once just like that beautiful child and therefore also able to provoke this love at first sight.

This is why I recommend that you keep the baby pictures of everyone in the family displayed around your house and office. And remember that you were once that newborn child entitled to everyone's love at first sight, too!

HOW TO MAKE THE MAGIC: Bring out the baby picture books of all of your children and of yourself as well. If you still have babies, make an extra effort to put even a modest book together—you'll treasure it later. Share the pictures with your family and talk about the memories from prebirth, birth, and infancy. Notice the affection and humor that moves through everyone with this experience, and try to renew this special connection often.

LOVE IS THE ANSWER

We are all born for love. It is the principle of existence, and its only end.

—Benjamin Disraeli

• • • •

Whenever I say "Love is the answer," I also ask "What is the question?" The truth is that love is the answer no matter what the question is. We are told to love our children and our enemies. We are told to kill with kindness and torment with tenderness. We are also told that love is blind to others' faults. All of these sayings recognize the true power and resonance of our love. We can create positive change through our effect on others and our love of them. Most of all what love does is let the person who feels loved know he or she is a meaningful creation who deserves to be cared for. One study found that adults who felt loved as children experienced only a fraction of the illness rate of those who did not feel loved as children.

We are not self-destructive if we feel loved; the love sustains us through it all. Every day, let your children know in subtle and creative ways that you love them. For example, place notes in their lunch boxes that tell them what adorable things you love about them and to have a great day. Teach them how to do fun things, such as baking a cake, in-line skating, working with clay or paint, or playing a new game. Spending time with them and gaining new experiences together is the best way to effect positive change in your children's lives and to show your love.

On the wall in our living room I have a portrait I painted of my parents, and beneath it are three messages: "I am because of my parents' love," "Enjoy yourself; it is later than you think," and "This too shall pass." Every time I walk by their smiling faces, I know their love is the answer and my love can be the answer, too.

> **HOW TO MAKE THE MAGIC:** Write the words "Love is the answer" on several pieces of paper, and place them where you work and around the house so that you'll see them every day. After doing that, whenever a problem arises in the family, ask yourself, "How can love be the answer to this problem?" After you answer the question, you are to go and act upon your answer. Eventually, I want you to stop anytime and anywhere, when you encounter a family member, and ask yourself, "If I truly love this person, how should I act now?" And do it!

GO TO "L"

The only reward for love is the experience of loving.

—John LeCarre

. . . .

No one will ever be upset with you for bringing the L's into their life: love and laughter. I have worked with many people dealing with life-threatening diseases, and I never heard any of them complain that I made them laugh or helped them to feel loved.

Bring the L's into your family life. Your children should be given the gifts of love and laughter throughout their lives, so that they can bring that joy to others as well. Make your children laugh with jokes, props, and toys. Spend some time each day asking everyone in your family about the fun moments they remember. Let them know you care about them through a hug or a story. Reliving the painful past does not solve anything, but enjoying the moment and feeling loved does. When you dwell on sadness and painful incidents, you are only prolonging negativity, guilt, and blame. Release these feelings, abandon your painful past, and concentrate on the L's.

How to Make the Magic: Have each person in your family come up with a comedy routine and perform it for the others. It can be a stand-up routine or a performance using some family experience as the basis for the new script. When everyone is ready, set aside a time, sit down, and enjoy the L's together. Believe me, these comedic moments will be remembered for a long time. (We still have these old videos and they are hysterical—*Saturday Night Live* at the Siegel household.)

MESSAGES OF LOVE

If we want a love message to be heard, it has got to be sent out.

—MOTHER TERESA

• • • •

As I mentioned earlier, after giving birth to three boys, my wife and I decided to give it another try in the hope that we would have a daughter. That's when we discovered we were having twins, and my wife came home and announced, "If it's two more boys, I am not coming home from the hospital." Thank God the first one out was our daughter, Carolyn! Then our obstetrician, Doctor Karlovsky, announced, "What a gentleman. He let his sister out first." So from Day One, our son Keith was a little angel who was always helpful and never a problem or troublemaker.

When the other kids had raffle tickets to sell, they gave them to Keith. With his angelic smile and demeanor, he would go from house to house and sell every ticket. We gave him the bedroom farthest from ours, at the end of the hall, because we never had to worry when his door was closed.

However, when Keith grew to be a teenager, he went through a period when he did not hesitate to let his parents know how terrible they (we) were. When he was away from home, he would call and leave twenty-minute messages on the answering machine telling us all the things we had done and were doing wrong. My wife would get very upset, but I would calm her down by telling her that he felt better after expressing himself. I told her our job was to love him, and that he left these messages because he cared about us and wanted to communicate his feelings of anger and frustration.

A few years ago, I mentioned to Keith that I still had the tapes of his phone calls. He said, "I think you can destroy them now." I said, "No, now you have a son, and someday he will call you and criticize you and it will break your heart. Then I want you to play your tapes and see that with love you can heal the family's wounds." He laughed and nodded in agreement. These messages remind us not only of the difficult stages in our relationship but also of the strength of our connection to each other. These messages allowed him to convey his feelings and allowed us to listen without any fighting and arguing.

HOW TO MAKE THE MAGIC: Call your child and leave a message of love for him or her. Talk about your feelings, whether they are negative or positive, so that you can remove any feelings of bitterness that exist. Encourage your children to call you and leave messages when they are feeling upset or resentful so that there is a constant channel of communication. When they know that it is okay to express their feelings, they will realize they are not being judged. These messages will help them know they can trust you and perhaps will even inspire them to come talk to you about what is troubling them, giving you an opportunity for understanding, forgiveness, and healing.

LOVE THEM AS THEY ARE

It is a great shock at the age of five or six to find that in a world of Gary Coopers, you are the Indian.

—James Baldwin

• • • •

Diversity is a common buzzword today. Everywhere we turn, from the classroom to the workplace, we are asked to embrace and advocate diversity. It's a wonderful sentiment, but it seems to fall on deaf ears as far as many kids are concerned. Teasing and rejecting other kids who look different—by birth or by choice—is as prevalent today as it was when I was a kid. For all intents and purposes, Jimmy Carter's notion of our "beautiful mosaic" seems to end where the school yard starts. Being different can make life very tough for a kid, especially when the difference is a physical one. Skin color, height, weight, nose size—all of these are fodder for ridicule, even when it is disguised as "good-natured" teasing. For kids whose physical differences are caused by physical disorders or birth defects, teasing and rejection, especially in the locker room, can feel particularly cruel.

What can we do to help our kids thrive despite other kids' thoughtless behavior? The most important thing is to show and tell them that we love them and are proud of them, exactly as they are. Let them know that their differences, including any disease and deformity, make them special and beautiful and have taught us important lessons about ourselves. And encourage them to be there for other kids who, like themselves, may be a little more "unique" than most kids are prepared to accept. I know kids who have died but are immortal through the effect they had upon those who knew them; their loved ones are now raising millions of dollars in their names to cure various diseases.

What if your eight-year-old daughter decides to dress like a boy every day and change her name to Buck? Or your teenaged son puts purple streaks in his hair, gels it into spikes, pierces various parts of his body, and gets tattoos in the remaining open spaces? What should you do now? Same thing. Let them know that you love them, even though they have chosen to express themselves in ways that you don't like. Some kids dress rebelliously to get attention; others may hope that by being bizarre, they will be left alone and won't have to socialize or relate to others—and some are just trying on styles to get a sense of who they are. The best thing you can do for them and for yourself is to simply accept them through their many phases of growing up. (If they are truly troubled, you may need to call on a professional therapist, but the key is for you to try to maintain as normal a relationship as possible.) With your continued love, acceptance, and support, your children have the best chance of finding a healthy and happy way to be unique.

HOW TO MAKE THE MAGIC: Give your kids a special one-week assignment: Seek out at least one schoolmate who is "different" and find something complimentary to say to him or her, without betraying the assignment. At the end of the week, ask them to share what happened, how they felt, and what they learned. If your kids are the ones who are "different," being supportive of others in this way can help decrease their self-consciousness as they increase their own sense of usefulness and worth. A distinctive appearance, after all, has put them in a unique position; they can help where others can't even understand.

UGLY DUCKLINGS

Always kiss your children good night—even if they're already asleep.

—H. Jackson Brown

* * * *

Think of the story "The Ugly Duckling." When he was born, he was seen as an outcast because of the way he looked. He felt isolated and lonely and had no confidence because of how others made him feel. Finally, he was able to see and accept the beauty in his reflection and become a swan. He had realized that what made him the ugly duckling was also what made him special.

I have always related to that story because I was born an ugly duckling. My mother had medical problems and was advised not to become pregnant. When my folks decided to take the chance and when her prolonged labor produced no results, and she was not thought likely to survive a Caesarean section, I was pulled out to save her. At that point, my mom said, "They handed me a purple melon, not a child." She and my dad took me home wrapped in kerchiefs and hidden in a covered carriage.

As I grew up, I learned my particular talents and uniqueness and became a surgeon, but this would never have happened without the love of my parents and my grandmother. The fictitious Ugly Duckling did not have the benefit of loving parents and grandparents. But when I saw myself reflected in their eyes, I saw someone who was beautiful and special. And, even though I was once an ugly duckling, I was able to bring beauty and love into the world through my desire to help others.

Let your children see themselves reflected in your loving eyes. All children are ugly ducklings at some point in their lives. Whether they are ten, thirteen, or eighteen, they will reach a stage when they feel awkward and ugly, or they may feel as if they don't fit in with their peers. Show them ways to develop their talents and their individuality. Tell them your own ugly duckling story. With your help, they will understand that even though it feels as though their ugly duckling stage lasts forever, soon their negative feelings will be a faint memory.

HOW TO MAKE THE MAGIC: Sit down with your children and tell them your ugly duckling stories. They may seem embarrassing for you at first, but eventually you will be laughing at those memories and your own insecurities at the time. Your children will get to see an entirely different side of you, and they'll be grateful that you have shared your own humiliations to alleviate their problems.

DO WHAT WILL MAKE
YOU HAPPY

*He that always gives way to others will end in having
no principles of his own.*

—AESOP

• • • •

Children want to please their parents, but a smart parent knows it is more important for children to make choices that please themselves. This is not about being selfish but about being authentic and not submissive. There are many reasons for a child to select a certain way of life or a career. It is tempting for a parent to try to sway a child to follow the direction the parent thinks is best for him or her. I suggest loving and letting go: Do not take your children's freedom of choice away by telling them what you have decided they are to become. Sometimes their decisions will be based on their birth order as well. The oldest child, growing up with the attention of two adults, is far more likely to become a professional than, say, a fourth child who grows up with other attributes due to his birth position, such as being comfortable with noise and with other people of all ages. With love and encouragement, however, any child born in any order can learn to follow her heart and make her own life decisions.

I hear from so many people who, when diagnosed with life-threatening illnesses, quit their jobs, redirect their careers, and go after their dreams. One patient I knew closed his law office and picked up his violin to become the violinist he always wanted to be. These people, of course, always benefit from reclaiming their lives and do not die "on schedule." They lost their untrue lives and saved themselves and their authentic lives. The words that explain it all go back to the biblical message "He who seeks to save his life will lose it, but he who is willing to lose his life will save it." When children give up their lives to gain the acceptance and conditional love of their parents, they have lost their lives as they could have been.

That is why, when people are seriously ill, they see with total clarity whose life they've been living; this awareness leads them to give up the untrue life and save their true self. At that point, they benefit emotionally, spiritually, and physically from the new life; they may even benefit from a spontaneous reversal of the illness. I fear, and studies reveal, that the child who lives her life to please her parents and internalizes her anger is also more likely to develop a serious illness later in life than the sibling who was a little devil.

> **HOW TO MAKE THE MAGIC:** Remember to repeat the following to your children often: "Being a success will not make you happy, but being happy will make you a success." When they have a decision to make, such as which activity to do, which college to attend, or which job to take, and they ask for your advice, remember there is only one right answer: "Do what will make you happy!"

A WISH COME TRUE

Tragedy and comedy are but two aspects of what is real, and whether we see the tragic or the humorous is a matter of perspective.

—Arnold Beisser

• • • •

What are your childhood memories? Are they about tragedies, or are they about moments of love and joy? I love listening to the stories my children tell, because the majority are memories they still laugh about or moments of love. And even though it is sometimes difficult to hear their painful memories, I still can enjoy listening because I know that these, too, are important shared memories and none of the pain was inflicted by the actions of members of our family. On the contrary, our family had a policy of turning all potential tragedies into comedies whenever possible.

I phoned one of our sons a short time ago to cheer him up and offer support following a painful operation from which he had not yet fully recovered. During our conversation, he recalled a late night in our family garage when he was working on his beloved car past one o'clock in the morning. An irate neighbor had called the house to complain, apparently assuming I would make my son immediately stop whatever he was doing. According to my son, the angry neighbor demanded, "Are you banging something over there?"

I answered: "We would be if you didn't disturb us by calling at this hour."

And my son carried on. The fact that he still enjoys sharing this story today proves that he appreciates my "turn tragedy into comedy" approach to child rearing. But there's more to it than that. My willingness to endure the wrath of the neighbors allowed him to fulfill his heart's desire at the moment, and that demonstrated my love for him.

In her poem entitled "Tragedy," Jill Spargur writes about longing for a red balloon as a child. They cost only a dime, but her mother wouldn't get one for her. "They broke so quickly, and besides she didn't have the time, and even if she did, she didn't think they were worth a dime." When the girl grows up, she has plenty of money and plenty of time, but she doesn't get herself a red balloon because "somehow, something died inside of me, and I don't want one now."

Don't let something die inside of your child. Try to help her realize her heart's desire, no matter how trivial it may seem. That doesn't mean you have to buy children everything they ask for, but if a child asks for one thing again and again, you can listen to him, acknowledge his wish, and try to help him make it come true. There are many ways to give children not what they want but what they need and desire: your love.

HOW TO MAKE THE MAGIC: Ask each of your kids to write down three wishes. Then sit down with each one individually and talk about his or her wishes. See if there is one that you can help your child fulfill right away. If not, try to find one you can help him or her work toward. Remember: Even their most outlandish wish may come true if it can be put in perspective. If your child wishes for no more homework, for instance, remind him that when summer vacation comes, his wish will be granted for three full months—and give him a small notepad to jot down ideas of how he would like to spend some of that free time. Help your children to find a place where dreams can come true.

LOVE, MAGIC & MUDPIES

SEND LOVE LETTERS
TO YOUR KIDS

Smile at your children, smile at each other—it doesn't matter who it is—
and that will help you to grow up in greater love for each other.

—MOTHER TERESA

• • • •

It's not enough to love your kids. You have to *tell* them that you love them. They need your love poem tattooed on their hearts so they can take it with them wherever they go. The famous poet Elizabeth Barrett Browning wrote, "I love you not for what you are but for what I am when I am with you." That's the essence of a family. Let your children know that their mere presence makes your life better every day and that they don't have to do anything other than be themselves to make the world a better place. That is what makes your life and theirs meaningful. Don't just say it; write it down for them. Words seem to carry more weight when they are on paper. Write love letters to your kids, send cards, and leave notes for them around the house.

Today, while searching through some desk drawers, I found a passage from a poem called "I'm So Proud of You," by Ruthann Tholen, that we sent to our children on Valentine's Day 1993. "When I held you as a child it was like taking up in my arms all of my hopes for the future," the poem begins. "I wondered then what you would become, and you haven't let me down.

"My child, you are a person to be proud of. You are sensitive, but strong, with the courage to follow your own path, to know and do what is right for you. The love between us needs few words, but is the foundation for all we give by being there, by sharing time and effort, by our talks, and by our caring. I'm proud when you accomplish things, but even prouder of the way you live. Whether you win or lose, you do it with dignity and integrity and humanity, and I respect that. From your own efforts, there has grown a deep goodness in you. I can wish nothing more than that your life will hold a future of happiness."

We signed each note, "I love you, and I'm very glad you are my child."

I can assure you that poem is going out again. I know our children will be pleased to remember when they first received it, and that it will encourage them and underscore how much they are loved as they face their own challenges with their families.

While you're spreading love around, be sure to tell all of your family members, your neighbors, and your kids' teachers how highly you think of your children and how much you love them. Why? Because the word will get back to your kids, and they will know you weren't saying it to them just to make them feel better. If you are telling it to everyone, they'll believe that you must really mean it. And they will be right.

HOW TO MAKE THE MAGIC: Get a book of poetry and find some meaningful poems to read or send to your children. Share them with all of your kids, whether they're still sitting in high chairs or facing them, feeding kids of their own. If you're having trouble with one, give him or her a poem anyway. Do it today. Then go through your calendar and make a note to give them another one on each and every holiday. After all, no matter what conflicts arise, they will always be your children, and you still have the right to love them, and they deserve to be loved.

WHO DID THAT?
CUT THAT OUT!

*Too often we underestimate the power of a touch, a smile, a kind word, a
listening ear, an honest compliment, or the smallest act of caring, all of
which have the potential to turn a life around.*

—LEO F. BUSCAGLIA

. . . .

How many times do we blurt out words in reaction to what our children have
done that upsets us? And how many times do we blurt out comments when we
are pleased and thrilled with what they have done? Do we put the same emotion
into words like "That's nice" as we do into "Who did that?" or "Cut that out!"

Well, I want you to rethink things and start a new policy. From now on, when you see
something nice that your kids have done, from a good report card or a clean room to a
promotion at work, I want you to bellow, "Who did that?" And when they come cower-
ing in response to your loud voice, greet them with a big smile and tell them how proud
you are of what they have done.

Here's another idea: "Cut that out" can refer to behavior that goes either way. But I want you to think of cutting things out of your life the way a sculptor does: You remove what's unneeded in order to create a work of art. You do this by helping your kids to cut things out and thanking them when they do, because they've enhanced the life of the family. There are a lot of things we can eliminate that will help us to focus on what is really important.

This reminds me of a story from Bill Cosby, about how his father would scream at him when he was out in the yard doing something that upset his dad. "Jesus Christ, get in here," his father would yell. To which Cosby would answer, "No, Dad, I'm 'God Damn It.' My brother is 'Jesus Christ.'"

HOW TO MAKE THE MAGIC: Try to think of some expressions whose meaning can go both ways. You will confuse the family when you say them. Then clarify them with a compliment for something they did. Here's an example: Bellow, "What in the world are you doing?" and when they hesitatingly explain, say, "I love it!" and give them a big hug.

SAY "YES" TO LOVE

Keep love in your heart. A life without it is like a sunless garden when the flowers are dead. The consciousness of loving and being loved brings a warmth and a richness to life that nothing else can bring.

—OSCAR WILDE

* * * *

The key to the lives your children will live is related to a very simple thing: what they hear you say "no" and "yes" to.

We have all heard the dictum "Just Say No" that was created to try to keep kids off of drugs. So why don't they say "no" when offered drugs or alcohol? The papers are filled with stories about college freshmen who drink themselves to death at frat parties. Why didn't they say "no" when they felt pressure to carry out self-destructive behavior? I believe that all addictions, from food to drugs, derive from a lack of love and a search for acceptance and feelings of satisfaction the children have never had.

So just what are you to say "yes" to? Love. Say "yes" to love, endlessly, because you can never say it enough. When our family talks on the phone or when we're together, we never part or finish our conversation without saying "I love you." Our sons have no problem with the "L" word, and that makes me very proud of them.

And what do you say "no" to? You say it to all of the self-destructive behavior that you are aware of in your children and in the world. Your "yeses" will help your children to say "no" when it matters. Make them aware they have choices and that with your love to support them, they will be able to walk away from destructive behavior and not worry about what other kids think of them when they refuse to get drunk or use drugs at some party. They will learn that you do not have to imitate others to belong when you already belong to a family that loves and accepts you.

How to Make the Magic: Say it loud and say it clear to your children and family every day of the year: "I love you." And when you see them thinking about, engaging in, or exposed to a lifestyle that is destructive or dangerous, say "no" with passion and compassion—not anger—so they know it comes from your heart. Remind them that saying "yes" to what is destructive is really saying "no" to themselves and their lives.

MOM, DAD,
HOW DO I LOOK?

Our society's strong emphasis on dieting and self-image can sometimes lead to eating disorders. We know that more than five million Americans suffer from eating disorders, most of them young women.

—TIPPER GORE

. . . .

Many are concerned about how our children perceive themselves and their appearance these days, particularly because of the media and its strong impact on the young mind. This has led to many questions, such as: How do you answer your kids, regardless of their age, when they ask you about how they look? Do you set guidelines and rules about how they dress? If you don't pay attention to your children's appearance, they may start believing that they are ugly beyond repair or you just don't care. They may try to go to extremes, such as plastic surgery, tattooing, or piercing, until they feel as though they have gotten through to you or received your approval—or sometimes disapproval, just to get attention. Remember, the opposite of love is indifference.

Your eyes are the greatest mirrors a child can have. Your words also reflect back to children what you see. Criticizing their appearance will greatly damage their self-esteem and may even cause severe body image issues in the future. Let them know how beautiful and handsome they are. You don't need a special occasion to say something nice, especially when they are not in the room but within earshot. When they hear you telling someone about how lucky you feel to have such beautiful children, it will get through to them, helping them survive the laughter and criticism of those who do not feel loved or beautiful.

Our children need to lovingly accept what they look like and not define themselves by what they think is wrong with them. By letting them know that you love them unconditionally and think they are beautiful both inside and out, you will instill a strong self-image in your children. On the other hand, try not to put too much emphasis on appearance. I always point out that our pets never spend time in front of the mirror or come and ask me for a bath and shampoo; they know they are here to love and be loved. We need to accept that the role of the body is to help us appreciate and enjoy life; it is not something to be used as a standard by which we measure and judge ourselves.

I once met a young woman born with no arms. I learned a great deal from her about wholeness and what we are capable of doing with bodies that may seem handicapped to others. The same is true of your children, who may feel they have no athletic ability or are not thin enough, pretty enough, or tall enough. Teach them to embrace life and to love their bodies despite any perceived imperfections.

HOW TO MAKE THE MAGIC: Ask your kids to draw a picture of themselves for you to use as a decoration. Then look at how much of the page they use and what their self-image looks like. It will tell you a great deal about their self-image and whether they need help or not. Take some time with your children to share the feelings you had when you were young about such issues as your appearance, weight, body image, and athletic ability. Ask them how they feel about their bodies, help them to love themselves, and help them to change what they don't like. Get them out walking with you or cook healthy meals in the kitchen together. Empower them with vigorous exercise, a healthy diet, a huge dose of self-acceptance, and lots and lots of love.

SPECIAL MOMENTS

Love is, above all, the gift of oneself.

—Jean Anouilh

. . . .

There may be many times when an opportunity for a special moment with your child comes and you let it go. As busy as you are, try to do everything you can not to let these opportunities slip by. Sharing those special moments will never be forgotten. I decided to celebrate my seventieth birthday by running my fifth marathon. Our son Jon decided to share the event with me. Instead of running in New York, which I usually do because I love the energy of the city, we chose to do it on Cape Cod, where there are hundreds of people and not tens of thousands.

Every now and then Jon would run ahead and leave messages with spectators to share with me, his dad, as I passed places he had been. I would find him waiting for me every few miles, too. When I recall the day, it leaves me with feelings that connect me to him in a very special way. Not only did it feel wonderful to be on the receiving end of such love, it showed me that our special moments of love throughout his life had taught him well.

It is incredibly important that, as a parent, you share these life moments with each of your children. These moments can be small, but they can change the course of your child's life.

How to Make the Magic: Share an event with your children, something very different from everyday life. It can be a chess tournament, a road or bike race, a walk in the woods, or another physical challenge of some sort. Learn a new skill or sport. Think of a creative or intellectual challenge, like solving a problem or building something for the family to use. Cherish the time together; you're creating moments that will never be forgotten.

PART THREE

TICKLING THE FUNNY BONE

If love makes the bricks out of which you build your life, laughter and humor are the mortar. Laughter and humor hold it all together, sustaining and repairing the weaker spots.

When you are serious and have to be right all the time, you spend your life in a prison confined by your fears. When you can laugh at yourself and be a child at any age, you are free. I know from my relationships, and especially my marriage, that our ability to laugh wipes out all the anger and returns us to the love we have built our lives upon. Honestly, if you had a choice, would you want to make war, make love, or tell jokes?

I once heard a story about a student who turned out to be Albert Einstein. His teacher asked the class if they thought evil existed. Einstein responded by asking the teacher if darkness and coldness existed. When the teacher said yes, Einstein discussed the physics of light and heat and said that it was their absence which we refer to as dark and cold. Evil, therefore, was simply the absence of God.

I would say that evil can also be the absence of love and humor. It is so important to include humor in your daily life. Try to come home every day with a humorous story or joke to share with your family, and leave the complaints at the front door. When you can laugh at the world, no matter what your age, you will find joy in living every day of your life.

CHILDLIKE HUMOR

Humor is the great thing, the saving thing. The minute it crops up, all our irritation and resentments slip away, and a sunny spirit takes their place.

—MARK TWAIN

• • • •

With all the worries and anxieties that absorb our attention, we sometimes forget that it's okay to stop and relax. We think that focusing on our troubles all of the time is the best solution to dealing with them. We forget that it is good to center ourselves with laughter and give ourselves permission to lighten up. There's no point in being serious all the time—worrying about the bills, worrying about our jobs, and worrying about our health. Worrying is the solution to nothing. We need to lighten up, and if we can't, how can we expect our kids to lighten up either?

Kids are quick to pick up on how we deal with stress. Knowing this, I always tried to do a few silly things to drive my kids crazy and get them laughing. What I basically tried to do was to act like the naïve child of the family. I did this in the hope of lightening up everyone's day.

For example, I might go into places where the sign said, "Nobody Allowed." When the security guards would yell at me, I would answer, "I am a nobody."

When I saw the sign "Wet Floor" in a hallway, I would say to our kids, "Let's do it!"

"Don't Throw Foreign Object in the Toilet" was one of my favorites. After I would come out of a public restroom, I would announce that I may have damaged the toilet. And when the maintenance staff would come running over to ask me what I'd done, I would tell them I dropped something from Italy in the toilet before I noticed the sign. (The unsuspecting people would never know if I was kidding or mentally handicapped.)

I would also complain about the baby changing stations because none of our kids ever improved their behavior after I placed them on the changing station. When we went to the pet store for supplies, I would always complain about the wild birdseed, saying I didn't want wild bird seeds and asking if they had any seed for tame birds. I also put a mailbox twenty feet in the air with the words "AIR MAIL" painted on it.

I could go on forever, but the point is about awakening your inner child. Why do I recommend this kind of insanity? Because your children will always have that silly and fun-loving part of you with them when they are out in the world on their own. When they are having a tough day and see the sign "Wet Floor," the day will get a little easier because of their immature and crazy parents. And when they are asked to "sign here" or "print your name," they will remember that it's always an option to write the word *here* or print the words *your name*.

HOW TO MAKE THE MAGIC: Make a list of crazy things you do at home, and start making plans about things you can do when out with the family. Become alert to the absurdities of the world and share them with the family through your sense of humor and freedom to be childlike. So when the elevator door opens and someone asks, "Going up or down?" or you hand someone your card to pay a bill and they say, "Credit or debit?" you know the right answer is "Yes."

LOVE, MAGIC & MUDPIES

SCHEDULE
LAUGHING SESSIONS

Laughter is an instant vacation.

—Milton Berle

. . . .

Let's face it. Raising a family isn't exactly all fun all of the time. The good stuff is amazing, but we also have to deal with illness, sadness, and emotional pain. I recently saw a bumper sticker that said, "Pain is inevitable. Suffering is optional." If we want to suffer as little as possible, we need love and laughter. Remember, bricks of love create the foundation for a good life, and laughter is the mortar that holds that foundation together.

Love and laughter are not just emotional outlets; they are proven physiological miracle workers. They heal us by changing our internal chemistry. Medical researchers have found that simply observing love can boost our immune systems. In one study, a group of college students was shown a gloomy movie about World War II while another group was shown an inspiring film about Mother Teresa. Blood tests taken immediately afterward showed a measurable increase of vital natural antibodies (immunoglobulins) in the students who watched the film about Mother Teresa. Another study revealed that even anticipating laughter jump-starts the immune-building process within our bodies.

Please use giant doses of love and laughter to keep your family healthy and happy. Schedule laughing sessions when you all get together and just start laughing. No reason is needed. Just laugh out loud and watch the effect it has on everyone. Get everyone to promise to laugh in front of the mirror every time they go to the bathroom. It doesn't matter if other people think you've all gone nuts. That will just give them something to laugh about, too.

HOW TO MAKE THE MAGIC: Try the movie experiment with your own family. Arrange a specific time each week to watch a funny movie together. Draw straws to give each person a turn to choose the movie. You'll get a double dose of health and happiness: when you anticipate seeing the movie and then again when you actually sit down and enjoy it together. The benefits will last a lot longer than the film itself.

LEARN TO LAUGH
AT YOURSELF

Laughter is like changing a baby's diaper. It doesn't permanently solve any problems, but it makes things more acceptable for a while.

—UNKNOWN

• • • •

Think for a moment about which you appreciate more: someone who criticizes your behavior and tells you to get serious, or someone who gets you to laugh at yourself because of something you said or did? I know my choice. For instance, I have no problem dressing outrageously at parties, wearing a wig on my shaved head, or suggesting that I go to a black-tie event in only a black tie.

So how can we get you to laugh at yourself when you are being the parent? In order to be free to laugh at yourself, you have to feel comfortable *being* yourself. When, because of my surgical personality, I obsessed about neatness by folding napkins or cleaning up crumbs, the kids always laughed at me. Their laughter helped me to relax as they often reminded me, "You're not in the operating room now, Dad."

If you try to see being a parent as something bound and dictated by certain behaviors and rules, you are in for big trouble. Being a parent is no different than being a child. If it becomes a set of rigid rules you must live by, life loses its joy and becomes a state of constant criticism. Talk with your mate, too, about giving yourselves some of the freedom the children have. Make fun of yourselves and your quirks so you can laugh and relax. The world is a serious enough place. Lighten up and be a joyful example to your family rather than a slave to the arbitrary expectations of conformity.

HOW TO MAKE THE MAGIC: Remember to relax and let the schedule go once in a while. Live in the moment and respond to your feelings and just get out of your own head. Ask the family to tell you stories about things you have done that made them laugh, and join in with their laughter. Above all, laugh at the things you do not know how to handle—you'll give your family lots of funny material just by laughing at yourself.

ONE-LINERS

If your parents never had children, chances are you won't either.

—Dick Cavett

• • • •

Parenting can be a tough job. Keeping a light and positive attitude will help bring some joy into a difficult time. One of my favorite ways to uplift myself and my family is to have a list of favorite one-liners that I use as needed.

When my wife and I used to lecture together, she would do a stand-up routine to help make people aware of how laughter improved their feelings, health, and well-being. I would introduce Bobbie by saying that we have had thirty-five wonderful years of married life, and thirty-five out of fifty wasn't too bad. Then she would get up and share some of our favorite one-liners:

"Don't go to bed mad. Stay up and fight."

"Sometimes I wake up grouchy and sometimes I let him sleep late."

"It's a good thing they sent a couple into space, so if they get lost, she'll ask for directions."

"When your husband asks if you can have dinner out tonight, leave a sandwich on the front porch."

And many more. To placate the men in the audience, she would finish with "But women aren't perfect. Three-quarters of all women can't understand fractions, and the other half doesn't give a damn."

Usually Bobbie received more thanks and compliments on her portion of the talk than I did. What impressed me was how the laughter literally changed the physical appearance of the audience. When she was done, they were all sitting up and looking alert and energized. Then I got to tire them out again.

I may add that the wise kids have one-liners, too. Our son Stephen was once upset with his four-year-old son, Jarrod. Jarrod ran into his bedroom, shut the door, and began yelling, "Don't you remember all the good times we had?" Stephen told me that he was so angry at the boy he yelled, "Son of a bitch!" Jarrod then yelled through the door, "What does that make Mom?"

Stephen had to admit that one-liner put a hole in his anger.

HOW TO MAKE THE MAGIC: Get a book by a comedian you enjoy, memorize some of the humorous material, and recite it to the family when you find a phrase or joke that really makes you laugh. Take your kids to the library and help them find some joke books, too. Rehearse and practice being a comedian with your kids. One day it will hit home how important laughter is to you and your family. One-liners always break the tension and heal the relationship.

USE ONLY ORGANIC FERTILIZER

Children are gleeful barbarians.

—JOSEPH MORGENSTERN

• • • •

Jon, our oldest son, is an attorney. He acted like an attorney from the time he was a child, and when you combine that with his Chinese birth sign, the rooster, you can imagine who was running the family the majority of the time. His siblings were glad when I came home from the hospital at night, providing them with relief from Jon's rules and regulations.

He shared with me one day that, when at a business meeting involving conflict between two groups, he used the expression he learned as a child: "Make them eat grass." Neither his associates nor I had any idea where that expression came from—until I asked the family.

His siblings said that when Jon didn't like what someone was doing, he would get them out in the yard, sit on them, and make them eat grass. He apparently often had help, depending on who was being asked to eat grass.

That is why I advise all parents to use only organic products in their yards and to be cautious about using pesticides; you never know when your children may be required to eat them.

Today my kids all laugh about it, but it just makes me wonder how we as parents can have so little knowledge about the world our children are living in.

HOW TO MAKE THE MAGIC: Check in often to see what your children are doing, especially when they are out of your sight. You never know what they may be up to while innocently "playing" with their siblings in the backyard.

SEX AND BABIES

Sex education may be a good idea in the schools,
but I don't believe the kids should be given homework.

—BILL COSBY

. . . .

Does this topic make you feel uncomfortable? If we as parents are not comfortable discussing certain subjects with our kids, then we may have a difficult time nurturing the inquiring nature of our children and properly educating them on certain topics. Children ask questions, and any subject—from sex, love, and baby making to violence and crime—may be open for discussion. The phrase "That is not a matter for discussion" should not exist in your household. If you have subjects that are not to be discussed in your home, your children will have to find other ways to learn the answers and cope with these issues, and they may end up with the wrong attitude towards "uncomfortable" topics.

Be honest and speak from your heart about your feelings and from your head about your wisdom, no matter what subject you may be discussing with your kids. Because I am a physician, my kids always turned to me for questions on anatomy. I remember our three sons standing next to the crib when we brought the twins home and asking, "Dad, how can you tell which one is the girl and which one is the boy?" I immediately gave them an anatomy lesson.

Educating our youth on sex, where babies come from, and other taboo topics helps to instill a healthy attitude towards these issues when they are older. I often went to my children's school, brought anatomy specimens to show the class, and helped the students to understand the human body. I was always impressed by the children's wisdom and interest.

If you are having a difficult time approaching your children, if something puzzles you or makes you uncomfortable, you can seek help from those who have been there before, such as your parents or grandparents. You can also go to the library with your child and do a little research or give them an informative book to read, such as *Where Do Babies Come From?* By being open with your children, you are giving them the support and knowledge to go through life making choices from a place of awareness, confidence, and encouragement.

Reminds me of a favorite joke: While out walking in their neighborhood, a man and his kids saw two dogs having sex, and when the kids asked Dad what the dogs were doing, he said, "They are making a puppy." One night, not long after, one of the kids walked into the bedroom while the man and his wife were making love. The son wanted to know what they were doing. The father said, "We are making you a baby brother." The boy looked disappointed and said, "Can you ask Mom to make me a puppy?"

HOW TO MAKE THE MAGIC: Teach your children about creation. Show them how plants, fish, and animals breed and create new life. Whether you use books or animals in the house as examples is not the issue. The point is to give your children the freedom to ask why and to become educated about life.

HOW TO SPY
ON TEENAGERS

It's a hard call, but I've no desire to live my children's lives.
I think my job as a father is to protect them, to allow them a safe place
to grow up, and to teach them what I've learned.

—ERNIE HUDSON

• • • •

We have four sons and a daughter, and all of the male voices in the family have a similar sound. So when we answer the phone, we are often mistaken for each other. When my kids were teenagers, this common trait gave me the idea to learn from my children without having to spy on them.

I would notice how they answered the phone using a trademark greeting such as "hi," "yeah," "hello," "what's up," and so on. I also made a note of their favorite expressions, like "cool," "that sucks," "way out," etc. Once I had done my research, I would often answer the phone by imitating one of my sons and deceive the caller into thinking I was him, in order to find out what was going on in my boy's life. I particularly enjoyed the technique when their girlfriends called. Of course, eventually I always let them know it was me, and we got a good laugh from all out of the attempt.

Now, you may think this is treading the line, but if the government can listen in on the calls of strangers, it seems to me parents should be allowed to tap into the lives of their children for their own sake, if necessary. I know many parents who sample their children's Internet use as well, and that is a wise thing to do.

This technique of imitating your kids will not work forever because your kids and their friends will catch on if you do it too often. So save it for times when you really have a question you need answered. And remember, sometimes a little spying can save your children from trouble along the way.

HOW TO MAKE THE MAGIC: If you're comfortable being a spy for the sake of your kids, give it a try: Listen to the way they speak on the phone, and rehearse your imitations until you and your spouse feel they are fairly good. Then start answering the phone and doing your under-cover work for the benefit of the family. It's all in good fun, and you might learn some great information this way. (And don't forget the Internet, too.)

YOU'RE NOT DIRTY
ENOUGH YET

Only where children gather is there any real chance of fun.

—Mignon McLaughlin

. . . .

O ur daughter always talks about how she remembers making mudpies in our backyard. I love building things, and our yard was full of many sandboxes, tree houses, and other structures I'd made out of wood scraps. I wanted the kids to have special spaces where they could create their own world. They'd fantasize about cooking meals, carving furniture, and playing with their imaginary friends and pets. I think we need to help our children see that the world is a playground and that they should feel free to make as many mudpies as they want to for as long as they want to.

Don't create a family that worries about how their clothes look, whether they have a stain on their pants or are dressed properly. If you are going to be making mudpies—and what kid doesn't want to do that?—what you are wearing doesn't really matter. It all comes out in the wash.

My own fun with mudpies came when I was a bit older. I was working in New York one summer as a page for ABC. During the lunch break, I would go to Central Park and join a baseball game in my page's uniform. I didn't worry about my appearance, or what my father would hear (he was an ABC executive who got me the job), or the results of the game—I was having fun making mudpies.

So let your kids go and make the biggest and best mudpies; they'll also be having the time of their lives.

> **HOW TO MAKE THE MAGIC:** Teach your kids that making mudpies is good for your health, and they'll never stop growing young. Whenever possible, try to dress casually and show your children that a little dirt or a hole in your play clothes is not something to be embarrassed about. Even in your professional life, try to lighten up a bit. I remember a multimillionaire who, after getting cancer, "cancelled the dress code" at work. No ties and no suit jackets from that day on. What's important is losing yourself in the moment of the mudpie—and you need to be dressed comfortably for that.

SET THE STAGE FOR COMEDY

God writes a lot of comedy . . . The trouble is, he's stuck with so many bad actors who don't know how to play funny.

—GARRISON KEILLOR

* * * *

I always enjoy looking at our old home movies and laughing at the silly things we did. My favorite clips are when we would perform routines as we imitated various comedians we saw on TV or in the movies.

Okay, the truth is, I just enjoy acting more childish than our children and grandchildren. I call them by the wrong names, from Clark Kent and Bruce Wayne to names I just make up; then I keep them busy as they try, intently, to tell me their real names. When I volunteer to serve lunch at their schools, I wear a rainbow wig and insist they answer my questions if they want food. Even the principal ends up sharing and laughing about the experience. It helps to make everyone's day a little lighter.

I also used to play Santa, dressed to the hilt like him, at the kids' school. I really enjoyed driving the students, who were our kids' friends, nuts with my knowledge of their personal lives and how if they didn't get along with their siblings, there would be no gifts this year. To teach the kids about anatomy, I would bring various organs to school. I always kept my talks light and informative, and years later some of them have brought me gifts to thank me.

Start rehearsals now; be the comedian you want to be, and give everyone a chance to display their talents. When you realize how much material every family creates, it gets easy. Make notes when something happens that gets everyone laughing so it can become part of the routine. Remember, life is a human comedy, and though it contains tragic moments, it feels a lot better when you focus on the comedy.

> **How to Make the Magic:** Set the stage for your family to become comedians; encourage them to tell jokes every day before dinner. While you eat, ask the gang if they have any funny stories to share and move on from there. Doing this will help them to focus on the funny things they experience each day, because they will want to remember them and share them that evening. It is a lot more likely for everyone to remember what went wrong each day. So start early training them to remember what was joyful.

GROW DOWN
AND LIGHTEN UP

When I grow up, I want to be a little boy.

—JOSEPH HELLER

• • • •

One of the best things you can do for your kids—and for yourself—is to make a point of staying young at heart. A great way to do that is to maintain a childlike sense of humor.

Don't hesitate to identify with your kids. When things go wrong, find ways to help them laugh at the situation without embarrassing them. Tell them a funny story about a similar accident you had or mistake you made when you were their age, and let them really get a good laugh out of it. That gives them an emotional "out" and keeps them from feeling pointless shame. Then be sure to tell them how you resolved the situation and learned to do better the next time. That gets them out of the problem and into the solution. Everybody wins.

Don't be afraid to embarrass yourself by acting like a kid. I am notorious for it. On Halloween, I would always put on a costume and sneak into a big group of kids so no one would recognize me. My neighbors had no idea it was me as I collected my treats with the rest of the gang. My kids thought it was hilarious when I dressed as a hunchback and actually scared dogs when I approached their houses. Serving as a Cub Scoutmaster provided even more opportunities to joke around with the kids, especially when I brought our unruly pets. They were a comedy routine in themselves. No matter what I said, they immediately did the opposite.

Humor isn't the only way to stay young at heart. My wife and I have kept our youthful attitude simply by keeping our kids' rooms intact, even after they grew up and left home. Just walking through the door and seeing their toys and books and decorations, exactly the way they left them, brings back a flood of memories and takes us right back to a younger age and time. That is therapeutic for everyone. And when our grandchildren come to visit, they get a big kick out of staying in their parents' old rooms and getting to see what they were like when they were kids.

> **HOW TO MAKE THE MAGIC:** Devote one full day to growing young with your kids. Share stories about your childhood. Show them souvenirs you've kept since you were a kid. Tell them the story that was your favorite when you were their age. Take them to an amusement park and go on all the rides with them. Don't just watch. Enjoy their childhood right along with them. When you get home, leave time for a nap.

EXAGGERATE TO CELEBRATE

Humor is a universal language.

—Joel Goodman

. . . .

The other day, our daughter Carolyn called. While her family was at Disneyland, her son became sick and they had to fly right home. He was very upset that he wasn't able to meet Winnie the Pooh, Piglet, Eeyore, or Tigger, and she wanted me to imitate them over the speakerphone for him.

When I started talking to him on the phone as Tigger, he immediately caught on that it was me. But as I got better at my impression, he calmed down and had a good laugh.

There are many ways to deal with difficult or traumatic emotional and physical problems, but a parent with a sense of humor will help the family get through them all. Once when we were stuck in traffic and the children were getting bored and agitated, rather than trying to soothe them with "Just a little bit more time, kids," I told them things were only going to get much, much worse. We had no food in the car, no toilet facilities, and it would be days before the traffic would start moving again. I joked that when they found our bodies, it was going to be extremely traumatic for our relatives. Well, it worked—they lightened up and started to get silly, too.

Exaggerate any part of the situation, and things will lighten up. For example, whatever anyone wants or expects, do the opposite. If you are in a restaurant and everyone thinks the meal is great or terrible, express the opposite opinion. If they want to go to the ocean, and you've been to the ocean several times already (and you can sense they're starting to treat it as an entitlement), drive them all up to the mountains for the day. Don't let your life become stagnant and routine.

HOW TO MAKE THE MAGIC: The next time the family is bored or troubled by something, assign someone the job of changing the situation by exaggerating the story. Encourage them to become some fictitious character who can solve the situation, like Spider-Man or Little Einsteins. If they are good at it, tell them to assign the rest of the family parts to play. This will lighten the mood and enable everyone to act silly, escape their comfort zones, and laugh at each other.

PART FOUR

CREATIVE PARENTING

I want this book to assist and coach you in practical ways and help you to become a more creative parent. But I do not want to provide a formula that everyone follows, making parents simply duplications of one another. Every parent has his or her own unique ability to be creative and apply it to raising a family.

When you create, whether it is a painting or a child's birthday party, you lose track of time and become ageless. As a parent, you need to appreciate your uniqueness and see your role as that of a creator. Your children are the raw material from which you are to help produce a work of art—a human being. The work never ends, and you can never fail. Just like a potter working a piece of clay on her wheel, the process of reworking and redoing can go on, gloriously, for a long time—indeed, for a parent, it goes on for a lifetime. Please remember that sometimes we learn more from the challenges and failures we have during our process of creation than we do when all goes well. And, just as with a painting or a work of clay, it is never too late to rework your creation.

As parents, we need to live and act in an authentic way so that we and our children can become unique individuals. When you base your life upon the effort to create, it will never feel like work. Being a parent gives you the greatest potential to create. So please see yourself in that role and not in the sole role of a disciplinarian who must get his family to follow a set of rules. Most of the world's geniuses and inventors would not exist if their parents had discouraged their creativity and uniqueness.

DON'T FORGET TO SING

The only thing better than singing is more singing.

—Ella Fitzgerald

• • • •

I love to sing songs with a message of hope, spirituality, and love. I may not be the greatest singer, but I am capable of singing one song in several keys. Growing up, I used to hear—and sing—"Somewhere over the Rainbow," and I loved hearing how my troubles could "melt like lemon drops" and my dreams could come true. *The Wizard of Oz* is a wonderful movie to share with your kids, especially if you encourage them to sing along and learn about the messages in the lyrics.

Another musical I always loved is *Carousel*. My favorite song was "You'll Never Walk Alone," about holding your head up high through a storm and not being afraid of the dark. It is full of heart and hope—perfect to share with your children.

A lot of songs can teach your children values, instill hope, and uplift their spirits. Some of my favorites are "You've Got a Friend," "The Impossible Dream," and "Amazing Grace." Most people don't realize that "Amazing Grace" was written by a former slave trader who saw the light when his prayers were answered and life saved and who spent the rest of his life fighting to end slavery. These kinds of songs are wonderfully inspiring, not just for us, but for our kids.

What songs do you sing to your kids each day? What lyrics will they remember throughout their lives?

How to Make the Magic: Delight your kids with a family karaoke night. You don't need all of the fancy equipment (though that can be outrageously fun, especially if the machine has a video component that allows you to tape yourselves in action). All you really need is a CD player or tape player and loads of music that you love. Pick show tunes your kids already know, perhaps something like "Circle of Life" from *The Lion King*. Then add a few they probably don't know but are sure to like, such as "High Hopes," Frank Sinatra's Oscar-winning theme song from the 1959 Frank Capra movie *Hole in the Head*. Go ahead, make some magic.

THE ART OF HEALING

*The symbol is the bridge between the literal world
and the direct experience of God.*

—Lama Govinda

• • • •

The important and meaningful things in our lives are at times best represented symbolically. When you have a dream, read a fairy tale, or draw a picture, you are connecting with a deeper wisdom and a truth that cannot be hidden. When a family tries to communicate and deal with life only through words, the family can become very good at denying and hiding the truth.

I know from experience, both with our children's drawings and those of my patients, how the truth spoke to me and helped me and other parents do the right thing. When I work with schoolchildren and ask them to draw their homes and families, I can quickly see how painful their lives must be when every family member is in a bubble and no one has ears to hear with.

By using children's drawings and dreams, I have been able to learn what is unspoken and help parents understand their children's needs. One little girl with cancer drew her family sitting on a sofa with an empty seat next to them while she sat alone on a chair. She said that she was not getting enough time from her parents and three siblings. The drawing touched them deeply and led to changes in the family's schedule and life.

Leave paper and crayons out and take a good look at your child's drawings. Learn from the colors and pictures how your child is feeling and what problems he needs help with. In our family, the kids started hiding their pictures unless they wanted my assistance in making a decision about something that was bothering them. (So, learn from my mistake here—don't tell them you are using their artwork for therapy, too!)

You could ask your kids to draw the answers to questions, such as: How do you feel about school? How do you feel about your brother (or sister)? What do you really want to be when you grow up? Or even, what college do you want to attend? By looking at their drawings about school, siblings, and choices such as professions or colleges, it is easy to see how your children would feel comfortable learning about themselves by talking about the scenes they depict. Another great benefit of this method is that it helps you understand how your children are handling their feelings when other members of the family are having significant difficulties as well.

You do not need to be an art therapist to understand and interpret some drawings. You'll easily be able to see that your child may feel confined to his classroom, or angry at a sibling, or trapped in a destructive friendship, or even feeling sorry for herself because of what she is going through. When the pictures show great conflict, it can indicate that something needs to be done to help your child to thrive and stay healthy.

Use your kids' art to tune in to how your family is dealing with their lives. This is not about critiquing their projects but about seeing what their hearts are feeling and responding to their often unspoken, but intensely felt, needs.

How to Make the Magic: To get the above process started so you can use it when there is conflict or an upsetting event happening at home, gather the family together for a fun-filled art session. Choose something simple for each of you to draw. You can pick a piece of fruit, the family pet, or a favorite toy. This is a playful process; remind them that this is not about judging the quality of their art but about being together and sharing time. Once everyone has warmed up and relaxed, see if they will move into drawings related to themes from which you can all learn, like the family, classroom at school, or a self-portrait. The only person who can properly interpret the drawing is the one who drew it. So share your feelings, but let the artist decide what leaving his parents' heads off means in his family portrait.

TELL STORIES

Stories are the creative conversion of life itself into a more powerful, clearer, more meaningful experience. They are the currency of human contact.

—ROBIN MCKEE

• • • •

When he was just a boy, future psychiatrist Milton Erickson was stricken with polio. As he lay in his bed, he heard the doctor tell his mother he didn't think her son would make it through the night. Erickson was determined to prove the doctor wrong, so he told himself a different story, in which he did make it through the night and saw the sun rise. He did survive, and his experience eventually inspired him to develop an entirely new approach to psychotherapy based on storytelling.

Erickson was a wonderful storyteller because he knew that stories affect the people who hear them—and can help them see what they need to do to resolve their problems. His "teaching tales" relied on questions, surprises, and an ample dose of positive humor to get people to see themselves and their situations in new ways. A child who was ashamed about having freckles, for example, became a cute cinnamon face in one of Erickson's stories.

The only thing more truthful than the truth is a story. The reason myths and fairy tales persist through the years is that they carry within them symbolic truths that touch us all regardless of our age. Yet, because they are stories, we can learn from them without feeling threatened or criticized. Even as a physician, I found it easier to discuss an anecdote or case history with other physicians to open their minds to things they had not been exposed to. When the presentation was over, they could leave saying "That was only an anecdote," whereas if I had presented statistics that threatened their belief systems, we would have ended up arguing about the validity of the research. I learned, in time, that they would show up with stories about other patients that they wanted to tell me about, and gradually our dialogue would evolve and our minds would open.

Stories are everywhere. We all have stories to tell. We can use them every day to help our children develop confidence and a strong self-image. I used a story about a plant that grew through the pavement to teach our children not to give up. If you really want to make your kids feel loved, "accidentally" leave this note addressed to your spouse on the kitchen table: "Don't we have the greatest kids? I am so proud of them. I know they will all succeed at whatever they do." Make sure you leave it on the table until all of your kids have seen it. This little storytelling praise will stay with them and give them confidence as they go out to face the world each day. That's what Erickson had in mind when he coined his signature phrase "My voice will go with you."

So read to your children, no matter what their age, and share the personal stories that have touched you and taught you about life. Make sure you also put the books aside and tell your story and what you have learned from it. Let your children do the same thing. Help their minds open by encouraging them to create fantasy worlds with heroes or heroines that they can realize represent them.

Besides the telling, have them write their stories and other stories they create. This gives them a chance to "try out" who they ultimately will become. They'll work their way through many characters, and the more they act out in stories, the healthier they will be in their real lives—they will not have to act out what they have already written out.

HOW TO MAKE THE MAGIC: Get the family together, regardless of age, from grandparents to toddlers, and have everyone bring their favorite story to tell or read. This special event can be done as often as desired, on a certain set day or evening. Hopefully, this tradition will make everyone more alert to what they see and hear, and teach them that every life is a story and that troubles can lead to happy endings.

Tell a story that will help your children get through the day and any difficulties they may face, physical or emotional. You can make up the story yourself or use one that you heard somewhere else, as long as it carries a positive message. You might want to tell a myth or fairy tale or talk about someone you—and they—admire. Think of Helen Keller's story, for instance. Her story can help everyone in the family. If she could overcome the obstacles of being deaf and blind to graduate from college with honors, there's definitely hope for your kids, too.

DIRECT TV

*By the age of six, the average child will have completed the basic
American education. . . . From television, the child will have learned how
to pick a lock, commit a fairly elaborate bank holdup, prevent wetness all
day long, get the laundry twice as white, and kill people with
a variety of sophisticated armaments.*

—AUTHOR UNKNOWN

• • • •

What would happen if we turned off the television set, locked it up, and threw away the key for three entire months? Nothing terrible, as it turns out. One of our sons and his wife don't let their three children watch TV during the summer, and the kids don't seem to miss it at all. If anything, they get more involved in other activities they enjoy, including outdoor sports.

Cutting down on the amount of time your kids spend in front of the television does not deprive them, particularly if you help them find other ways to channel their energy.

Banning TV altogether does not mean that your kids will automatically make better use of their time!

Think about this: All of us are essentially TV sets, satellite dishes, and remote controls. Our worlds offer infinite channels, sounds, voices, and distractions that we can choose to tune into or ignore. Our minds are the remote controls that constantly click on various channels as we go through each day. What we see and hear becomes what our faces and bodies display, just as a TV screen reveals the program you select with your remote control. You know how discombobulated you feel when one of your kids surfs through the channels at breakneck speed, never stopping long enough to really see what any one program is about? Is it at all surprising that you have the same feeling when you allow your mind's "remote control" to do the same thing with the millions of "channels" of your outside world?

The best thing you can do, for yourself and for your kids, is to stop the endless channel surfing and focus on one thing at a time. What matters most is what they watch and how much time they devote to it. Concentrate on channels that display the lifestyle and wisdom you want your kids to enjoy. Are crude humor, violence, and "reality" shows the reality you want for your family? Help your children—and yourself—select the proper channel to tune in to on TV and in their own lives.

HOW TO MAKE THE MAGIC: Become a TV director. Sit down with your kids and work out a meaningful policy that reflects your reverence for life. Steer them to the type of shows you want them to see, and set firm limits on the amount of time they are allowed to watch. Ban all programs that are violent or destructive. (While you're at it, think about getting rid of violent or vulgar computer games as well.) Try to help your family understand that you are doing this so that all of you can be better people and enjoy life more.

GREEN PARENTING

If we raise our children so they are orphaned from nature, unable to feel comfortable and live in productive harmony with nature, then they will be at the mercy of technology. But if we can give them a reverence for the earth and a confidence in their ability to live in productive harmony with nature, then technology will fit easily into a total, interrelated approach to life.

—James Hubbell

• • • •

As a parent, when your child enters the world you want him to have a wonderful future. But do you ever stop and think about what you put into your child's body and environment? Just look at the increase in autism and the research that has been done relating it to mercury in the environment and possibly to your child's vaccinations. Parenting becomes more complex now that a parent can no longer be sure the water, air, and food are entirely safe.

As an informed adult, you should stop and think about the appliances and bulbs you purchase and how much energy they will use. Certain fuels, which are burned to produce energy, pollute the air we breathe. Certain food additives contaminate our food supply. When you buy products, read the descriptions related to energy use. When you are at the grocery store, read the labels to see what ingredients are in the products you are buying for your family.

As your children grow up, teach them to be aware of these things, too, from the advantages of organic foods to avoiding fish that contain mercury. Take them on hikes and bike rides so they can appreciate nature and green life. Teach them about the value of a tree and the importance of taking care of the environment.

Clean out your cabinets, remove toxic products, recycle, and reduce waste. Show your children how to compost. Explain how these actions will make a difference for generations to come. Instill a reverence for all life into your children.

The most vital factor is to practice what you preach and be an example for your children. When I jog or bike ride, I carry plastic bags with me and collect cans and bottles discarded on the side of the road by uncaring people. One day, I was frightened when a police car pulled up in front of me and two officers jumped out with their hands on their guns. Then I heard one yell, "Oh, it's Siegel." I am now in the police records, which made our children very proud of their father, because a woman called in to say a bald man was running away from her house with a bag full of stolen items. Of course it was my collection of cans and bottles.

HOW TO MAKE THE MAGIC: Explore the many different ways you can help the environment and create a green household. Pick a site in the backyard for a compost pile and get the family started using it. Buy secondhand furniture and clothes to reduce consumption of material goods. Study various sources of energy with the kids, like the wind or sun, and consider having alternative sources installed in your home or on your property. Look over your home and come up with ways to make it fuel efficient and free of toxins. Have your family shop together, and read labels to make healthy choices. You can enjoy life and still be a green parent.

CHILDREN'S DAY

Our time is the single most important gift to give our children!

—LEE-ANNE ROBERT

* * * *

How come we have Mother's Day, Father's Day, and Grandparent's Day, but no Children's Day? Why don't we set aside a day to celebrate our children? Now some parents may think they are entitled to be recognized and honored for surviving the experience known as parenthood, but I truly feel our children need to be honored, too. Sometimes we forget to appreciate our children while they are young. I believe there are more ninety-year-old parents who would want to celebrate the gift their children have been to them, while many thirty-year-old-parents are ready to board their kids in a kennel for a week's vacation the way they do their pets.

One of our five children reminded me today of how I would take them on trips and to special events individually and show my appreciation and share in their interests one at a time. When our drummer son and his band, Panacea, would perform, I was always surprised by how few parents of the other band members came to hear their children play.

By appreciating and enjoying the time I have spent with my children throughout their lives, I am able to look back on all the wonderful memories that I have shared with them.

Make sure you honor your children and their uniqueness. I know the reality of raising children, but I also know they need to feel that they are special and different. Go ahead and create and name a Children's Day—perhaps it will catch on and be a time that is treasured! To honor our twins, who were born on December 26 and therefore often had their birthday and gifts co-opted by the holiday celebration, we created a second birthday party celebrated every June 26 to which all their friends came bearing gifts.

> **HOW TO MAKE THE MAGIC:** Sit down with your kids, no matter what their ages, and ask them when they would like to have an annual Children's Day to celebrate with you. This does not mean you will stop spending individual days by sharing time and doing something special together. This is not to be used for material gift-giving. This is a day for spiritual, life-enhancing expressions of your love for them and the unique experience they are for you.

LOVE, MAGIC & MUDPIES

A TRUE EDUCATION

Education is not the filling of a pail, but the lighting of a fire.

—W. B. YEATS

• • • •

Today's world is filled with information, but very few children get a true education. How many of us feel like we grew up prepared for life and its difficulties? And how can we prepare the next generation for what lies ahead?

The first thing to teach your children is that their mental health and physical health are inseparable. Because your child cannot live an emotionally satisfying life without encountering the world outside the classroom, you need to understand that there are experiences that may provide a better education than attending school. Your children need to educate themselves in their own time. For example, whenever our children displayed an interest in something such as sports, music, or animals, I would help them pursue that pastime and encourage them to educate themselves about the subject they were interested in. If they wanted snakes and turtles, then they had to study these creatures, join herpetology societies, attend meetings, and read books about them.

When one of our sons started building models of World War II planes and tanks, he became an expert through his reading and work. I would stand back in amazement when we went to hobby shops, where he would get into involved discussions with veterans about the topic. I was never able to join in these conversations because I did not have his technical expertise. It's no different when cooking, collecting stamps, playing soccer, or playing an instrument becomes a new enterprise for a child. Support your children's interests, and help them to grow and to learn through new experiences that they have chosen. Of course, there will be times when you think that their obsession with eighties music is a bit annoying, but through these pastimes, they are able to develop their own unique personalities.

HOW TO MAKE THE MAGIC: Get involved in your children's hobbies; help them to pursue them, and become knowledgeable about them, whether their interests are animal, vegetable, or mineral. Encourage them to read about and study the subject, investigate it online, or join a club of people who enjoy the same topic. You never know where it may take them in their lives that their years of schooling couldn't.

HEALTH DAYS

*Sometimes the best medicine for children is to let them
make their own decisions.*

—Unknown

. . . .

One dilemma parents often face is deciding whether their child is really ill or just "faking it" to get out of school. When our children stayed home due to illness, as a physician, I would write very detailed absence notes that contained scientific medical terminology. I would write notes describing specific bacteria and anatomical areas of inflammation and more, knowing the teachers would get a kick out of my craziness. I even received a reply from one teacher thanking me for getting her to smile in the morning before classes began—something, she said, that is very rare for a teacher to do.

To allow our children to have days off and not have to pretend something was wrong, I gave them health days instead of sick days. I wanted them to be aware of the fact that they didn't have to be sick to take a day off and just enjoy it. So every semester they were entitled to a week of health days, and all they had to do was say, "I'm taking a health day today." No questions were asked. What this did was take their focus off of being sick and put it on responsible self-care. Today many people take this type of time off and call it a mental health day.

Your children may have days when they need some time to recoup from their busy schedules and lives. Even though they may not be technically "sick," they may need some time for themselves to just enjoy being children. Understanding their needs and letting them know that they can relax and take it easy from time to time will also give them more incentive to work hard, secure in the knowledge that there is time for fun and rest always available. It is a good habit to teach them for when they become adults and parents and need to remember to take time to relax and have a "health day," too.

Health days are not just for your children; they are something to put into your schedule as well. Parents most of all need times to rekindle their spirit, rest their nerves, and take a nap! Set aside days off to just do nothing and work on your own mental health.

How to Make the Magic: Consider setting up a plan so your children can take health days off from school as the need arises. You can give them a number of days that they are allowed to be absent and tell them that these days can be used for health or sickness purposes. Notice how the days they miss for "sickness" suddenly diminish.

MUDPIES AND MUDSLINGING

When life gets down and dirty, jump in and make mudpies!

—Michelle Wade

• • • •

Children and animals are capable of finding joy and becoming playful with whatever is at hand. They do not whine and complain about what is missing in their lives—at least not until they are teenagers. They create with what is at hand. As parents, we need to follow their example; we need to dig into the mud of our lives and watch what magic happens when we start to use it creatively.

We can experience the darkness and hard times, live in them, and feel despair. Or we can change our response to them, taking our charcoal and turning it into diamonds under the pressures of our life. We can sling mud at others, become mired in it so that we cannot walk or drive ourselves forward. Or we can plop down, become creative, and make mudpies and build castles.

I have seen people use earth, mud, and sand to create beauty through what they have designed. The results are truly works of art and came originally from the simplest of materials. Take whatever issue or problem is at hand in your life now, think of it as your mud, and use it to create a pie. Use clutter or extra materials around the house to create your works of art.

I personally never throw things away—from car parts to broken toys—and love to use them to build things for our children and pets to play in or with and to decorate our yard and the trees around our house. Yes, our house looks a bit strange. But by building mud-pies, or sculptures, or whatever project I design, I remain creative and keep my life energy flowing. It helps me to be a better person and a better parent.

HOW TO MAKE THE MAGIC: Collect toys, tools, and equipment—all the odds and ends you're certain don't have another use left in them. Then one day get the family together for an outdoor art day and see what you can create from all the items you have accumulated. We have bird feeders and birdhouses made out of plastic jars, metal paper-towel dispensers, and wood scraps in our yard. (As I wrote this, I looked out the window and saw ribbons, balloons, and artificial flowers that came on gift packages decorating the landscape, not to mention old road signs.) When tensions mount with your children, in the family, or in yourself, gather together your art supplies and create a special project.

LOVE, MAGIC & MUDPIES

TAKE YOUR CHILD TO WORK

As adults, we must ask more of our children than they know how to ask of themselves. What can we do to foster their openhearted hopefulness, engage their need to collaborate, be an incentive to utilize their natural competency and compassion . . . show them ways they can connect, reach out, weave themselves into the web of relationships that is called community . . . ?

—Dawna Markova

• • • •

Sharing your life with your family includes sharing your work or profession. When you show your children that you like your job and you take pride in what you do, it allows them to see the many possibilities for their futures. Every one of our children spent time making rounds with me at the hospital and came to watch me at work in the operating room. I wanted them to share my life and experience so they would get to know and understand me better.

When I was a young boy, I can recall going to work with my dad and sitting in an office my father gave me for the day. I had a desk, phone, paper, and pen and could act like an executive all day long. I especially enjoyed when people came into the office looking for some executive and were bewildered by the child sitting behind the desk.

The kind of job you have is not the issue. The point is to show your children a part of your life that they usually do not have access to and how you relate to people through your work. They will be thrilled to share this occasion with you and to take part in something they have never done before. I remember how excited it made me when my father would say that we were going to the office for the day. Make this time together fun, as well as a learning experience. Also, let them know that you want to share time with them—and not because you want them to follow in your footsteps.

Let your children see how you interact with people and things at work, so when you come home in the evening, they will know what you have experienced and why you may need some time to relax before getting involved in family situations. Your children will become more understanding of you and your work once they get to know the places and people you have to deal with on a daily basis.

How to Make the Magic: Talk to your kids and find out about their school schedule and what holidays they have off. Or decide to take a special day off for this occasion. Then invite them to spend a day with you. You can even take them out for a business lunch that day and make it something special for them. (You can either do this on the national Take Your Child to Work Day or on another day—which might make it even more special.) Do not let the gender of your child alter what you offer them in terms of sharing your work. Our daughter was more at home in the operating room than our sons, some of whom grew faint, while she stared into the wound. You never know who will be interested in what area or career.

MOVE IT

Busy hands make happy hands.

—Unknown

. . . .

One cannot separate movement and development. I was recently listening to someone share her experience treating children and adults with various issues, such as ADD (attention deficit disorder) and recovery from stroke, using movement therapy. She gets these patients to relive their developmental stages, which enhances the functioning of their brains, similar to that of a developing child.

She was speaking about how, in our society, there are so many seats for infants or children to sit on or be caged in that they do not get a chance to develop their motor skills and ability to react with the environment both visually and physically. She believes that when we began to encourage parents to have their infants sleep on their backs, to decrease the incidence of sudden infant death syndrome, we also saw an increase in ADD. Once again, their ability to react to the environment was limited and, thus, so was their development. I can see her point; I think we need to explore all of these factors and not just respond with drugs to every affliction a child experiences.

Children need to crawl, creep, and develop their ability to move, make eye contact, and be touched by people and their environment. Many children are restless, aggressive, and self-destructive because they need to be violent to feel anything. They've never had any meaningful contact, so they do not develop the receptors for these joyful sensations. As a result, even pain is preferred to numbness. They cannot appreciate the pain they cause others because they did not have an experience of feeling loved when they were growing up.

The point of all this is to get your kids moving—and feeling and touching—from the day they are born. Watch them and keep them safe, but also give them the room to move their bodies, look around with their eyes, and explore. These are the skills they will need to relate to people who are physically close to them and to read and observe others' expressions and appearances.

> **HOW TO MAKE THE MAGIC:** Try to devise ways to help your children move, depending upon their ages. Do not restrain them in child seats that do not allow them any freedom of movement. Even older children who are restless or have attention problems can benefit by lying on their stomachs and creeping and crawling again. Do not hesitate to experiment with movements, dance, and sports so your children can develop physical skills and become coordinated and prepared for what life puts in their paths.

WHAT'S COOKING?

Cooking is like love. It should be entered into with abandon or not at all.

—Harriet van Horne

• • • •

How would you feel if you asked one of your children what was really important for parents to know and do and your child answered, "Learn how to cook"? Well, that happened to me, and I loved the answer. It really struck me that cooking was a creative act the family could do together. The son who answered my question is now an exceptional chef and treats his parents to many wonderful meals. Even today, he helps teach me how to creatively prepare and cook food, something I was never very good at but find interesting and enjoyable.

Years ago, when the kids were younger, we would spend evenings painting together. I think cooking is also an artistic expression and should be something families occasionally do together to express themselves and to have fun. Look at what's cooking in your life and get everyone involved in it. Whatever your interests or hobbies, share them. It can be changing a tire, fixing a faucet, making a dinner, painting a wall—anything that you are called upon to do around the house. I framed a piece of cardboard the kids had placed their paint cans on when they were helping me to paint. It looked like a famous abstract painting because they spilled so much paint on it in so many interesting patterns.

When you get together to create something, you nourish your family life. These times together will remain a constant reminder of your love and a unifying force for all involved.

HOW TO MAKE THE MAGIC: Get the family together and decide upon a meal that everyone would enjoy. Then assign members to help create the meal. You can divide up the components, like soup, salad, main dish, veggies, dessert, etc., and have a team or individual for each part. Then set the date and go shopping together, come home, and create a meal you will never forget—no matter what it tastes like. (Remember you can always go out for a bite if the timer wasn't set and the fire in the stove filled the whole house with smoke.)

THE RIGHT THING TO DO

*Nearly all men can stand adversity, but if you really want to
test a man's character, give him power.*

—ABRAHAM LINCOLN

. . . .

If you really want to know what your child is like, give him the freedom to make decisions. Allow your child to choose the right thing to do, particularly when he has hurt someone or something by his actions.

When your child comes to you and shares something that disturbs her, ask her what she thinks is the right thing to do. If you see an upsetting or injurious act and choose to do nothing about it, you are training your children to do the same. Likewise, you are setting an example for your children when you choose to make a positive difference, such as when you decide to clean up someone else's pollution or rescue an injured animal. Even watching you hold a door open or help someone carry her groceries are all actions that will ultimately determine what kind of a child you are raising.

Your children have to feel free to act in the way they think is proper. If their first thought is about what someone else will think or say about them, then they may never take the steps necessary to rescue or help another living thing.

The US Marines teach survival behavior, and one of their instructions is "Do the difficult right over the easy wrong." Whether they grow up to be marines or CEOs, when children grow up with parents who are committed to consistently emphasizing right action towards all living things, abuse and wars will cease. We need to prepare our children to benefit the world with the power they have. Make sure your children do. Our children have the power to love, and I would not worry about turning over to them the right to make a decision as well.

HOW TO MAKE THE MAGIC: Create a situation, then discuss it with your child asking him or her to decide what is the right thing to do to resolve this problem. You can make up a story about something that happened at work or use a real family dilemma, but give your child the responsibility to decide. You will learn about your child with this exercise, and chances are, you'll develop newfound respect for his or her compassion or problem-solving skills.

ART, LITERATURE, AND MUSIC

A musician must make music, an artist must paint, a poet must write, if he is to be ultimately at peace with himself. What one can be, one must be.

—ABRAHAM MASLOW

• • • •

Most of today's parents tend to get very involved in how their children are doing intellectually, while often ignoring the development of their creativity. How will you know if you are raising the next Mozart or Michelangelo? Have you ever asked one of your children's teachers if they think your child is sensitive, thoughtful, and creative versus smart?

Many evenings when the kids were little and I was busy painting portraits, I would include our children and we would all paint together. I did this so they could have an opportunity to be creative, as well as to spend time together. If children are exposed to visual arts, music, and writing while they are young, the parts of their brains involved in these activities will develop more fully. You may also discover that they were born with special talents. This practice and these new capabilities will act as resources for your children, should they want to pursue these skills as adults.

The fact that something doesn't interest you is not a reason to shut the door to your child's world and opportunities. You may also find that there is a talented child in you who was never given the chance to wake up and come out of hiding, because you were so busy doing what others wanted you to do and found no time to create. In today's technology-oriented world, we need to find ways and time to bring forth our children's creative energy rather than let them sit and play computer games without utilizing other resources. Tell them that by developing their creativity, they just might create far more entertaining computer games someday rather than mechanically playing them now.

HOW TO MAKE THE MAGIC: Set up an area for painting in your home, get the necessary supplies, and then gather the family together. Place some fruit, an object of interest, or a family pet before you and have everyone paint what they see. When you're done, share your paintings and hang them in your home. Another idea, when your children are young, is to have a blackboard and colored chalk available. Or collect some drums and start a drum circle while those who can play other instruments join in. Or even have a writing workshop. Everyone writes a short story about something of interest to him or her or some meaningful experience. When you have all completed your work, set aside an evening for everyone to share their creative endeavors with the family. When you do this, the world you live in will become more interesting to all.

MONEY TALKS,
BUT CHOCOLATE SINGS

A day without chocolate is a day without sunshine.

—Anonymous

• • • •

Most of us have handled our basic needs of food, clothing, shelter, and water, and we have the resources with which to obtain them. But after those are taken care of, what else makes us and our families happy?

Everyone has their particular joy in life, that certain something that makes them happy in a meaningful way; I call it their chocolate. As parents, we want our children to grow up educated and well-rounded, but we sometimes forget to ask them what they are interested in. Instead we try to decide what they *should* be interested in, what they should practice or learn. The necessary items, such as school, homework, and chores, are nutritious, like fruit or vegetables, and we want to make sure they have these things to keep them strong and healthy. But we also want to make sure that they have things that interest them, such as sports and the arts—this is the "chocolate" that makes them smile. So ask your children what their chocolate is. What makes them happy and creates a feeling of fulfillment for them?

A fourth-grade teacher who's a friend of mine forwarded me an e-mail from a parent complaining that his daughter was doing her homework and not practicing her guitar lessons. The father wants her to play the guitar and is totally against homework. The sad part is he has no idea what his daughter prefers to do. It is sad because he is not asking her, "Honey, what would make you happy?" Depriving your children of their own preferred chocolate, whether it is homework or horseback riding, keeps them from having a truly happy childhood.

How to Make the Magic: How can you get your children to find their chocolate? Watch them when they have free time and observe what they do, what they read, what they watch on TV, what games they play, which family vacations they enjoy the most, and what they do when they are with their friends. Talk to their teachers, not just about their grades, but to see if they know about their other interests and talents. Once you've discovered what moves your kids, help them to follow their areas of interest in any way you can. And don't forget to help them try new things every once in a while, to help them expand the offerings in their own chocolate boxes. Remember, this is *their* childhood, not yours.

PURPLE

by Alexis Rotella

In first grade Mrs. Lohr
said my purple tepee
wasn't realistic enough,
that purple was no color
for a tent,
that purple was a color
for people who died,
that my drawing wasn't good enough
to hang with the others.
I walked back to my seat
counting the swish swish swishes
of my baggy courduroy trousers.
With a black crayon
nightfall came
to my purple tent
in the middle
of an afternoon.
In second grade Mr. Barta
said draw anything;
he didn't care what.
I left my paper blank
and when he came around
to my desk
my heart beat like a tom tom.
He touched my head
with his big hand
and in a soft voice said
the snowfall
how clean
and white
and beautiful.

PART FIVE

THE THREE R's—RULES, REGULATIONS, AND RESPONSIBILITIES

We generally think of the three R's as related to reading, writing, and 'rithmetic. Now, these subjects certainly are important, don't get me wrong. But they are about information, and information can't change lives without inspiration. In this book, our three R's—rules, regulations, and responsibilities—relate to the lives of the people involved and not just what they know.

Having rules, regulations, and responsibilities for your kids shows them that you care about them. When you demonstrate the fact that all of our lives involve the three R's, you make a connection with them. As a teen, would you feel more loved by a parent who asks as you leave home, "Where are you going tonight? Who is going with you? How are you going to get there? When can we expect you home?" Or would you feel better if, as you head out the door, your parent says, "See you later," grunts, or says nothing at all? Setting specific boundaries will help your children to feel loved.

I can never leave home without my wife saying, "Drive carefully." This is her rule for me, and when she says it, I know she loves me and cares about how I drive because it relates to my safety. Self-destructive behavior is not tolerated by those who love you. None of our children smoke because they are loved and know how their parents feel about smoking and how bad it is for their health. (I wouldn't stop loving them if they did smoke, but I would say, "Not in my home or in my car.")

Why do I want our children to have responsibilities? For many reasons. The more responsibilities and connections to the world you have, the longer you live and the healthier you remain. When you create children who feel responsible for the health and well-being of others, you create a healthier world for all of us to live in because we all parent each other and feel close to one another. Not a bad idea and not really that hard to do. One main thing to remember: These three R's must come from a place of love, not from a place of fear of punishment, guilt, or shame.

CONSTRUCTIVE CRITICISM

Raising kids is part joy and part guerilla warfare.

—ED ASNER

• • • •

Negative criticism generates guilt, shame, and blame. Parents should always try to talk to children in a nonjudgmental manner and use constructive criticism, coaching, and feedback, which improves children rather than making them feel defective or that there is something wrong with them.

When children grow up with constructive criticism and do not have to make excuses for their behavior, they learn to apologize and move on. Those children will live very different lives than the ones who felt they were the problem. These poor kids never understood that it was their behavior or lack of knowledge, not themselves, that was the real problem.

When you need to correct your child, try to start the sentence with "What you did was . . ." and tell her why her behavior was inappropriate. Your child will see that she needs to act differently in the future, but that you still love her and she is a valuable person. If you begin with "What's wrong with you?" or "You are a bad girl!" the child begins to feel as though she is worthless and that *she* is the issue. Her actions begin to point to the fact that she thinks she cannot do anything right because there is something wrong with her. By creating a boundary between her behavior and her self-identity, you can maintain a strong self-image for your child.

I let our children know I wasn't perfect, and I welcomed their advice about how to be a better father. I also tried to be an example and apologized when I hurt or disappointed them with my behavior or my lack of availability due to the demands of my life as a surgeon. As I have said, I also took them to the hospital with me, just as my dad took me to his office when I had the day off, so they knew I was proud of them and that I wanted everyone to know our children. This opportunity to "show them off" helped my kids create a positive reflection in their own mirrors.

How to Make the Magic: Let your children know that you love them even when their behavior is inappropriate. Remember to use positive reinforcement and constructive comments to help them learn that they are not the problem, even when their actions need to be reprimanded or changed. You can love a child whose behavior you don't like.

NONDIRECTIVE THERAPY

All children behave as well as they are treated.

—Jan Hunt

. . . .

Many years ago, when our five children entered their teen years, I was thrilled to have them go off to college or some other place of interest to help restore some peace and quiet to our household. Our second son, Jeff, had many interests, but leaving home was not one of them. I kept encouraging him to do what would make him happy and pursue a career or further education, but he seemed to enjoy staying home. I even promised financial support if he decided to go to college.

The following year we got him, very reluctantly, to go off to college. I spent the day just getting him and his things into the car, and we arrived at the admissions office five minutes before it closed for the day. At college he received only two grades. If something interested him, he got an A, and if it didn't, he ended up with an F. He lasted there one year and then returned to his bedroom.

At this point, I knew I had to get the message across that I expected him to go out into the world and make his mark. So one afternoon when he was away, our youngest son and I dismantled his bed and hid it. This is known as nondirective therapy. I was not yelling at or criticizing or pressuring him, just dismantling and hiding his bed. That evening at bedtime, his siblings and parents stood in the hall, awaiting his reaction. There was none. He simply went into his room, shut the door, and did not make a sound.

The next morning he came to the breakfast table and said, "Thank you. My back feels much better." I learned from that experience that nondirective therapy is not terribly effective. It did, however, make a point with a bit of humor. He knew he was loved and was not offended by our gesture. After a bit of time, he drove away from our Connecticut home in the middle of a blizzard to join his brother and go to school in Denver. I am sure he did that to get even with us, knowing we would worry about him!

Nondirective therapy must be done with humor and the knowledge that your children understand you and your way of doing things. The key is to let your children know that you care about them but that you think they should change a certain aspect of their behavior. They will eventually get the hint and see that they need to take control of their lives and modify their actions on their own. Having our son, who played the drums, live downstairs was a way of letting him know the noise he made was affecting the entire family. It is never about taking control of your children's lives but helping them to find their own direction, and that is why it is nondirective therapy. How they respond is up to them, but at the very least, you will all get a laugh out of it over the breakfast table.

HOW TO MAKE THE MAGIC: Try to think of a humorous way to let your child know there is something you would like him or her to do or be aware of. It can be a letter or card you send, something you put in their bedroom, or a phrase you paste on the bathroom mirror, such as "A creative mind is rarely tidy" or "Dull children live in immaculate houses." Just let the message come from the child in you to the child in them.

LOCK 'EM UP

When my kids become wild and unruly, I use a nice safe playpen.
When they're finished, I climb out.

—ERMA BOMBECK

• • • •

When kids are naughty, parents often choose to give them a time-out. But what do you do when they are not being naughty, yet they are so energetic that they could run out in the street in the blink of an eye? My wife and I had to literally lock our kids in the house.

Our first three children came one at a time and basically got into as much trouble as any kids, on their own, as a team, and in conflict with each other. I had to continually enlarge the house and build extra bedrooms to try to keep them apart. Then the twins came along, and a new level of dangerous and destructive creativity was reached. They could practically read each other's minds, so they were a formidable team. They were able to get into trouble beyond their brothers' wildest young dreams. They could ascend to new heights because one would help support the other as they climbed onto furniture or over railings I had set up. They could unlock doors the others couldn't even reach. It became evident that I would have to take extreme measures just to keep them safe.

One day I realized that in order to provide them—and us—with some sense of security, I would have to make our house a place no one could leave. So I placed locks and bolts on every door, high above any spot they could reach even when helping each other to climb up onto dressers and chairs. I even nailed a piece of plywood across the bottom of their doorway so we could see in but they couldn't get out. I wasn't trying to keep anyone from getting into the house, but no one was going to find it easy to get out.

One of the partners in my surgical practice stopped by to visit one day and said our house reminded him of a war bunker. Our neighbors were somewhat skeptical. Plumbers and other workmen went crazy trying to navigate the place. But I felt secure knowing that my children were safe. Robert Frost said, "Home is a place that when you go there, they have to take you in." I say home is a place that when you go there, you can't get out, unless it is safe to do so.

> **How to Make the Magic:** Take action to make your home a safe place. Look around your house and yard. If you see anything that is a potential hazard, remove, replace, or repair it. If you don't notice anything hazardous, let the children loose for a day and keep a close eye on them—they will go right to the equipment and areas where they enjoy risking their lives and health.

SAY UM-M-M
IN FIFTY-THREE WAYS

I have found the best way to give advice to your children is to find out
what they want and then advise them to do it.

—HARRY S. TRUMAN

• • • •

As parents, we typically do a lot of talking. We tell our kids what to do, then ask them why they didn't do it. We talk to them about the facts of life. We argue with them about doing their homework, then sit down and help them finish it. We talk to their teachers. We talk to their friends' parents. We talk, talk, talk.

But what would happen if we took more time to listen? I have learned from experience that listening to people accomplishes a great deal more than telling them what to do. I remember hearing psychotherapist Larry Le Shan say, "If you want to be a good therapist, learn to say 'um' . . . in fifty-three ways."

I decided to test his theory before following it through with my kids. Before, when one of them would come to me with a problem, my usual tactic had been to start by telling them what I thought they should do. My recommendations were, of course, based on my own experience. Imagine how shocked and disappointed I was when their answer was "Dad, you're no help." Having failed miserably at that tack, I then went to Plan B, as suggested by Dr. Le Shan. I kept all of my sage advice, experience, and wisdom to myself and instead just sat and listened for twenty minutes with an occasional "um-m-m-m," "hmm-m-m-m," or "uh-hum-m-m-m." To my surprise and pleasure, they finished their monologue with "Dad, you were a great help. Thank you."

Helen Keller said that deafness is darker by far than blindness. My experiment with listening to my children showed me that when I did all the talking, I may as well have been deaf as far as they were concerned. They may as well have been sitting in a dark room, talking to a wall. But by listening to them share their stories, I allowed them to hear themselves for the first time. They were able to better understand their own feelings, so they could make their own good decisions, based on their own experience.

HOW TO MAKE THE MAGIC: Write a note to yourself tonight and put it up in your bathroom where you will see it when you get up in the morning. Just put one word on it: *Listen.* Leave it there to remind you to spend the entire day listening to your family. Ask them questions, such as "How are you feeling?" or "What's on your mind?" or "Anything you want or need to talk about?" If they respond at all, just practice your um-m-ms and listen.

THE PROBLEM CHILD

Life affords no greater responsibility, no greater privilege,
than the raising of the next generation.

—C. Everett Koop

. . . .

In my opinion, too many kids are on prescription drugs today, not because they choose to be, but because they have been branded as having various psychiatric disorders. Some of these kids do have problems that may call for medication, but many of them may actually be suffering from more common issues, such as undiagnosed allergies, challenges at school, or difficulty coping with daily life. Those kids may get more harm than help from psychiatric drugs. And I am sure all of them would benefit greatly from a huge dose of understanding and attention. We need to respond to their experience and not to a diagnosis.

Do you know when your children are having problems? How can you determine what is causing them? Two words: *Pay attention*. Watch their behavior carefully; try not to assume that they are simply being obstinate or that it is "just a phase." My son Jeff used to hide in a big cedar closet all day rather than go to school—and I didn't even know about it because he did it only when his mother and I were out of town. Our other kids lied to the older couple staying with them, so the sitters believed Jeff had just gone to school early. When I returned, his teachers and psychotherapists told me that Jeff had a "school phobia," so, as a dutiful father, I took him to a psychiatrist.

Decades later, I finally learned the truth. I asked Jeff what he did in that closet. I was amazed by his answer: "I read books all day." He wasn't afraid of school. It bored him. If I had paid more careful attention, I might have discovered that fact and been able to work with his school to give him more challenging assignments. On the other hand, if I had gone along with the school authorities' diagnosis without seeking another professional opinion, they might have prescribed totally unnecessary drugs to treat him for a phobia he didn't have.

Sometimes kids have medical problems that go undiagnosed because their behavior is written off as mischief. Our twins were born after Bobbie was exposed to German measles during her first trimester of pregnancy. When they were old enough to go to school, they got in trouble for not paying attention and being disruptive in class. At home they would often turn the TV up extremely loud and fight with each other. Bobbie thought they might have a hearing impairment, but our pediatrician said that they were just distracted. Bobbie insisted on having their hearing tested, and she was right.

HOW TO MAKE THE MAGIC: If your child seems to have a problem, investigate it thoroughly. Don't accept the first diagnosis or prescription that is offered, especially if you have a hunch that there may be another explanation. If you can, see a holistic physician who will consider everything from diet to emotions. The last thing your child needs is a quick diagnosis and prescription without anyone taking the time to be sure what the problem is. As a parent, you know your child better than anyone, so speak up. Our daughter's son Jason has many health problems, and she uses her phone camera to document Jason's progression, to show doctors pictures of when problems start and the sequence of his symptoms. This helps them to see that she often knows what is best for him from past experience and helps to get them to change their decisions.

ANIMAL AND CHILD TRAINING

Train up a child in the way he should go, and when he is old,
he will not depart from it.

—PROVERBS

• • • •

Our family has many pets and wants to raise them properly, so we've bought books to provide us with information on their behavior and how to train them. We also subscribe to *Cat Fancy* and *Dog Fancy* magazines, and I've always thought we could use a magazine entitled *Child Fancy*. Think of it: a magazine to help parents raise their children through the time they are taken off the leash, uncaged, and allowed their freedom. It could handle all the biggies: housebreaking, socializing, behavior, aggression, play, you name it.

In my opinion, the key factors in raising pets apply to kids, too: love, trust, respect, and consistency. We need to live by these virtues. If we are responsible for our behavior, our children will learn responsibility. If we forgive, they will be forgiving. Both children and pets learn from what they experience in their lives. Of course, love is the most important thing we can give them. And yes, rewards and treats can play a part, too, and should not be forgotten. As the Dog Whisperer recommends: exercise, discipline, and affection!

Getting down into our child's world will help. We are more likely to kneel down to our pet's level while we hover over our children to show them we are the boss. Nine hundred years ago, the Jewish physician and philosopher Maimonides said, "If people took as good care of themselves as they do their animals, they would be saved from many illnesses." Children belong in this equation as well; care for them, appreciate them, and be unconditionally grateful for the joy they bring into your life (even when they jump on the couch or make a mess or otherwise act like unruly pets!).

HOW TO MAKE THE MAGIC: Take a look at the ways in which you have trained your pets. Are they well trained, or do they run amok throughout your home? If they are well trained, what type of discipline, rules, and rewards do you use to keep them happy, respectful, and well mannered? Can you apply these principles to raising your children? When you have a well-defined system, with clear rules and responsibilities, everyone knows the behaviors and policies of the home.

If your pets run wild, see if this correlates with your children's behavior. If so, look at the way in which your household is run. Start by creating a list of rules and rewards, obligations and responsibilities. Apply this list to both the animals and the children. Or better yet, have your children train your animals—both will learn responsibility. Everyone wins! And remember to post the list on the kitchen wall. Then the list is the problem and not you.

THE VALUE OF PETS

The only members of your family you get to choose are your pets.

—BERNIE SIEGEL

• • • •

We live on a dead-end street that ends in a circle. Our home is in the center of the circle with other houses, so we have some privacy. On our one and a half acres of property, we have had a yard full of dogs, goats, ducks, and geese. Inside the house we have had every furry animal you can name, from squirrels and de-skunked skunks to exotics like monkeys and kinkajous. We also had an assortment of reptiles, and in our son Stephen's bedroom was a dead tree where various lizards and chameleons resided. There was also a cage with his "Monty" python. We were never reported to the police for breaking the zoning laws, and when we occasionally had to ask the police to keep an eye out for a missing animal, they never cited us either. However, needless to say, getting babysitters to stay in the house was not easy.

It was stressful at times for me to play the surgeon by day and veterinarian by night, but it helped our family learn many lessons. Multiple studies show the health and life-extending benefits of owning a pet you feel responsible for. A pet will provide your child with unconditional love, help him learn to relate to other living things, and, when the inevitable comes, teach him how to deal with the illness and loss of loved ones as well. I could go on forever. One list of "proper behavior" that I read at some of my lectures ends with "and if you can do that, you're almost as good as your dog."

When your child agrees to feed and walk the dog, for instance, and does not keep his promise, this is a good time to teach him consequences, not only for his behavior, but because of what would happen if the dog went hungry or without exercise. This way the child learns the outcomes of cause and effect and how his behavior can greatly affect another.

Violent behavior is not something your children will feel comfortable with if they grow up loving and caring about other living things. When children learn to feed and care for pets, they learn how to be responsible, feel compassion and reverence for life, and share with another living thing—in short, how to be complete human beings.

HOW TO MAKE THE MAGIC: Consider adopting a pet, preferably a "rescue" from a shelter. To help make the decision and after you bring the pet home, have family meetings about how to care for the animal. Provide your kids with reading material about the specific pet's needs; discuss everyone's role and responsibilities; and stress the importance of love, trust, respect, and consistency in raising pets. Even the youngest family member can be responsible for something small, like changing the water in the pet's bowl. Be sure to give positive reinforcement when the jobs are well done.

BECOMING A GOOD PARENT

By the time you learn to be a good parent, you're out of a job!

—UNKNOWN

. . . .

You know the way to Carnegie Hall—practice, practice, practice. Being a good parent requires the same effort. And relatives, friends, and all types of coaches are there to encourage you and help you practice until you get it right.

Work is necessary to achieve anything we hope for. If life is a labor pain, then why don't we have birthing classes that can truly prepare us for the experience? When you are about to become a parent, you can enroll in all kinds of classes to help you with the birthing process—but then the classes end. I want to know why we don't have more parenting classes. Think about it. What if every insurance company made it a part of their policy for you to take parenting classes after the birth of your child or they wouldn't pay any of the medical expenses related to the birthing process? They would save a fortune because a child who grows up loved has far fewer illnesses, addictions, accidents, and criminal behaviors. We can learn from the wisdom of those who have preceded us. We don't have to learn from our mistakes. I think we need to be truly educated in how to love ourselves and our children, and not just informed about how to change diapers or bottle-feed or breastfeed a child and all the mechanics of the task. We should also be trained in touch, communication, nutrition, exercise, and all the fundamental aspects of great parenting.

HOW TO MAKE THE MAGIC: Go to a playground and, after observing everyone for a while, talk to the parents you admire and learn what you can from them. Then talk to the seniors in your family and ask them what they wish they knew beforehand that they ended up learning the hard way after they had a family. Love may always be the answer, but there are a lot of other bits of advice that will help you all get to Carnegie Hall by the short, easy route.

IMAGINE NO POSSESSIONS

My riches consist not in the extent of my possessions,
but in the fewness of my wants.

—J. BROTHERTON

• • • •

Whenever I hear a recording of John Lennon singing "Imagine," I wonder if many families are able to see themselves in the way he imagined the world—a brotherhood of man living with no possessions, living a life in peace. My family certainly wasn't that way. Not most of the time, anyway. One of the most common words shouted by children from the time they are old enough to speak is "Mine!" I think a loving family may see more of this because the kids know they are accepted and can explore boundaries. As an example, one of our sons collected underarm antiperspirant bottles. His room was always filled with them. Not mine to question why. Years later I discovered, eavesdropping on stories our kids were sharing, that these were his ammunition. If anyone invaded his space, the bottles came flying at them and the intruders always retreated.

All people, including parents and children, sometimes become possessive about what they believe to be theirs, from toys, tools, and other belongings to their private space. Kids are famous for hanging "Keep Out" signs on their doors; those who share rooms with siblings are territorial about their beds. This is natural and normal, but it can become harmful if it causes conflict too much of the time or overshadows the love that holds your family together.

How does your family feel about possessions? If you moved to a smaller home and had to eliminate a lot of your belongings, what would you be willing to give up? How about if you stayed in your present home but had to cut down on your personal space and belongings in order to have more room for family activities? What would you be willing to give up for the happiness and security that the change might bring to your children? We parents need to ask ourselves this question at least once a year, as a kind of spiritual spring-cleaning. It reminds us that we do not own our children, and what we do own— our personal space and belongings—does not define us or make us happy. What we families really have is love, and that cannot be enjoyed until we share it. Our hearts reside in our treasure chests, which hold our one truly meaningful possession.

HOW TO MAKE THE MAGIC: Sit down with your family and discuss the things that are important to each of you. Talk about how you would feel and act if you had these things taken away. Discuss every item until you get down to what you want your children to know they will always possess: your love. Be sure they know they will have that no matter what, even when they do things they are not supposed to.

IS LIFE FAIR?

Being a mother isn't simply a matter of having children. To think that is as absurd as believing that having a piano makes one a musician.

—SYDNEY HARRIS

• • • •

The three most often repeated words of virtually every childhood are: "It's not fair!" You've heard it muttered under your child's breath, shrieked at a decibel level that could wake the dead, sputtered between clenched teeth, and sobbed in desperation. Sometimes it may be an excuse or an angry protest, but other times it is a genuine expression of pain, powerlessness, and confusion. How can we guide our kids through those difficult times?

I remember talking about this with Norman Vincent Peale, who wrote *The Power of Positive Thinking.* (His book has sold more than twenty million copies and has been printed in forty-one languages.) I shared how my mother drove me crazy as a kid because I would pour my heart out to her and she would simply say: "It was meant to be, dear. God is redirecting you. Something good will come of this." I hated hearing those platitudes. I always felt that she just didn't want to deal with my problems. Dr. Peale told me that when he was a kid, he also would tell his troubles to his mother, and although her reply was similar to my mother's, it offered him hope in language that any kid could understand.

"Norman," she would say, "when God slams one door, further down the corridor another door opens." Now you can see why he wrote a book about positive thinking. What else could he do, with a mother like that?

I'm not sure I would call my parenting approach "positive thinking." I just try to keep things in perspective, and the result is generally quite positive. For example, when I ask kids if they think life is fair, almost all of them yell, "No!" Then I tell them that it must be fair, judging by their unanimous response—all of them are complaining. Life is difficult for everybody, therefore it is fair. After all, "fair" doesn't mean everybody wins; it just means we all get a spot at the starting line. After that, life is full of slammed doors, redirections, and various varieties of labor pains. Perfect? No way. Fair? Absolutely.

Your kids need to hear that, even if they don't want to. They need you to show them how to get through life's aches and pains without letting other people dictate how they should feel or react. Keep your personal power—don't give it away to anyone or anything—and teach your children to do the same. As a mother, if you "write a prescription," remember that your kids don't necessarily have to fill it.

HOW TO MAKE THE MAGIC: Have faith in life's corridor of doors. Give your kids the freedom— and the power—to make their own choices and pay their own consequences. How do you do that? Share your own experience with them. Tell them about a mistake you made when you were their age and demonstrate how it taught you to do things differently the next time. That will give them courage to risk making mistakes of their own. Ask them what is most difficult for them right now, and then share your experience with a similar dilemma. Encourage them to try their own solutions, knowing that you will be right there to catch them if they fall. That gives them the power they need to be successful. If you stand in the way and try to stop them, you will get run over. So move to the side and offer directions.

WORDS OR SWORDS

Children have more need of models, than of critics.

—JOSEPH JOUBERT

• • • •

When our son Stephen was young, he often brought home some of his artwork that he had done at school. One piece I remember particularly well was a large canvas covered with the word *words* repeated endlessly with no space between the words so they became "swordswordswords." That hit home for me, as a parent and doctor, how powerful words can be to the self-esteem of a child. I realized you can harm or heal with words, as well as scalpels or swords.

As a parent, you often have the opportunity to use words to help heal your children on many levels. You may find that in the frenzy of trying to raise children and keep a house, a job, and a marriage going, your words come out in haste. Be aware of the reaction, effect, and response you receive from your children. It is never too late to let them know you did not mean what you said. Choose words that offer praise over criticism, empowerment over shame, and your child will grow up better prepared to live a secure and productive life as an adult. The written word can have just as strong an impact as the spoken word. A kind note left in their lunch box or pasted to the refrigerator when you're not home can mean a lot.

And don't forget to tell them as often as possible the most wonderful words of all—*I love you.*

HOW TO MAKE THE MAGIC: Think about how your verbal and written communication affects the health and well-being of your family. How can you give them, and yourself, constructive messages? Practice speaking in a positive way when you greet each member of your family. Remember to use those loving messages for speaking to yourself as well.

TO SPANK OR NOT TO SPANK

Never raise your hands to your kids. It leaves your groin unprotected.

—RED BUTTONS

. . . .

Our five children—including twins—were born within seven years, so things got a bit hectic at times. Occasionally I would lose it, shouting and threatening everyone within earshot as I dished out orders about how they were to behave and live. Their standard response to their surgeon father, whether I was ordering them around or organizing like a fiend, was "Dad, you're not in the operating room now." That usually quieted me down or got me to appeal to my wife for help. She was a kindergarten teacher who knew how to work with, live with, and raise children.

I'll never forget the day I came home from the hospital and she told me I needed to fence in the backyard.

"Why do we need a fence?" I asked.

"Because we have five children and they're running all over the place," she replied. "It's hard to keep track of them." I couldn't understand what was so difficult.

"A caring mother shouldn't have a problem watching her children," I pronounced.

That weekend my clever wife told me she had some shopping to do and left me with the kids. I got to see for myself how smart they were, ganging up and running in opposite directions to escape. Needless to say, the next day I had a fence installed.

The kids also were very smart when it came to handling me when I would get into my threatening mode. Although I rarely, if ever, spanked any of them, I occasionally found myself on the verge of losing control when my wife had left me in charge. I didn't hit anyone, but I did raise my right hand as if I were going to swat the behind of whoever was driving me crazy. Our oldest son Jon would say, "Go ahead and hit me. It will hurt you more than it does me." And off he would walk, and, yes, he is a lawyer today. That made me pause, but the experience that truly stopped me from even thinking about spanking ever again happened while we were away on vacation one year. I was very angry at our next-oldest son, who was about seven at the time. I was chasing him around the kitchen, and when I finally caught him and raised my hand to spank him, he said, "You can't hit me."

"Why can't I hit you?" I asked.

"Because I'm a person," he said smugly, "and if you hit me, I'll call the police."

I laughed so hard it cured me from any further desire to spank him or any of his siblings ever again.

> **How to Make the Magic:** Take a look at your children and see them as people. They are not yours to command or punish. Treat them with the four necessities: love, trust, respect, and consistency. Proper coaching and occasional rewards get far better results than constant destructive criticism.

TABOO TOPICS

*If parents and kids can talk together, we won't have as much
censorship because we won't have as much fear.*

—Judy Blume

• • • •

The topics of substance abuse, sex, and violence are important to confront in an open manner with your children. Keeping topics "taboo" or off-limits makes your child's curiosity stronger, and they will eventually learn about them anyway. So, create a way to talk to them about these subjects that is not preachy or judgmental. Instead, make yourself accessible and give them the knowledge that these things are a part of life and the world we live in.

Letting your children know that violence exists, but that it is not an acceptable behavior or expression for them, is a good way to help them understand the true nature of the world and also their role in it. The best way to do this is to be a positive example for them. By loving your children, you will show them that love, not violence, is the answer. Because they feel loved, violence will not become an issue or a solution of choice when they have problems. My father never raised his hand to spank his children. For me, knowing how caring he was, it was very upsetting to hear my mother say, "I am going to tell your father what you did when he comes home." I would then bargain with her and offer to do anything so she would not tell him what I had done. There are many ways to interact with the world that are more powerful than violence. Try to kill with kindness and torment with tenderness.

Sex is also a tricky subject to confront with your children. As a physician, when I tried to explain our anatomical and sexual differences, I always found it humorous to hear the kids mispronounce various body parts. Having at least one girl in the house helped so they could see the differences as they bathed together in the tub when they were small. The key is to get over what went wrong with your sex education and just jump in and bring the topic up. The kids are getting information from many places, and with today's computer access and porn, who knows what they are seeing before you even think about discussing it with them? So get in there and discuss it in a healthy way, and set your limits, too; but most of all, make communication easy for them and let them know you are ready to talk about sex at any time.

The temptation to use drugs and alcohol will become a part of their life, but when children feel loved, they will not need to abuse substances in their search to escape from pain.

> **HOW TO MAKE THE MAGIC:** Arrange to have a "taboo topics" night or meeting time where the subjects to be discussed have to do with substance abuse, sex, and violence. If no one has anything to say, you can sit in silence or bring something up that you as a parent wonder about. If you do this, the silence will be broken at some point; believe me, I know. Also, please make sure everyone knows humor is okay, too. Our son-in-law often sends me jokes that have inspired me to call him my "sin-in-law." I am glad he is comfortable doing this, because I know it opens the door for us to discuss many issues.

LET THE KIDS
BE THE PARENTS

The parents exist to teach the child, but also they must learn what the child has to teach them; and the child has a very great deal to teach them.

—ARNOLD BENNETT

. . . .

O ur third son, Stephen, spent so much time with his older brothers that they basically became his parents and teachers. One was three years older and the other was five years older. When Stephen was three, our whole family walked to the corner where his older brothers would catch the school bus for the first day of school. When they got on the bus, he tried to follow them as he always had when they played together at home. But this time, my wife and I had to stop him.

We walked home and Stephen was in tears the entire time. I realized that his brothers were more important to him in his daily activities than his parents were. They were truly his role models and teachers. And the truth is they did a really good job raising him. At times they seemed more concerned with his behavior and safety than my wife and I seemed to be. When they were too restrictive out of concern for his safety, he would come to me, knowing I would give him more freedom than his brothers did.

So lighten up and let them learn from each other. You may have forgotten what it feels like to be a child, but they certainly haven't. Let them learn from each other how to interact with people. It's one of the greatest blessings of having siblings. I could always tell the size of our babysitters' families by how they handled our children or how our children handled them! When my wife and I would come home from a movie and find the babysitter sitting on the couch staring into space while the kids ran all over the house, I would always ask, "You're an only child, aren't you?" And when another babysitter was on the floor acting like one of the kids, I would ask, "Do you come from a large family, too?" Of course I was always right.

How to Make the Magic: Prepare your kids for life by letting them prepare each other. Give them responsibilities and opportunities to share their wisdom with each other. If you have only one child, make sure he is involved in groups with other children his age so he can share in a family experience.

PART SIX

ROCKY ROADS—TROUBLES ALONG THE WAY

I survived a great many disappointments and obstacles because I remembered the wise words my parents shared:

> *This too shall pass.*
> *Enjoy yourself—it's later than you think.*
> *God is redirecting you.*
> *Do what will make you happy.*
> *We are here to make life easier for one another.*

These are all wonderful words of truth to help guide us over the rocky parts of our life path. As I began to write these words, I recalled developing arthritis in my fingers just as I finished seven years of training as a surgeon. All I could imagine was that my career was over and I would have to redirect my life, which included three young children and a wife. I was also about to enter the army as a physician. Well, the army told me they didn't want a disabled surgeon, and so I returned home to figure out what to do. Upon returning home, I found that the arthritis disappeared and became a wonderful redirection, freeing me from military service and leading me to the beginning of a career in surgery.

Prepare your family for life's difficulties and emphasize that life is not unfair—we all have our share of stumbling blocks—but those who carry a compass and a spare tire can get to their destination even after they lose their way or have a flat. It is up to you to provide your children with the tools to repair and support their lives and the beacon with which to light their way.

THIS TOO SHALL PASS

Tough times don't last . . . tough people do. Everything shall pass, your sadness or your laughter. When you encounter problems or difficulties, just remember these four words: This Too Shall Pass.

—UNKNOWN

. . . .

A king asked his advisors to come up with a motto that would help him get through tough times. All of his wise counselors shared their sayings; however, the king did not feel any of them were beneficial. One day an old man wandered through the castle, and the king happened to ask him if he had any words of wisdom to share. He said, "This too shall pass."

We have to realize that the longer we live, the more losses and disappointments we will experience. Teach your children that no matter how sad, depressed, or angry they may feel, it will pass, life will continue, and they will experience happiness again. Teach your children to be survivors, because those who believe in their ability to survive will spend less time suffering and grieving.

HOW TO MAKE THE MAGIC: Review your journals and the family history of your closest relatives. Ask them to share with you the personal, financial, medical, and commercial events that they did not think they could manage or survive. Then ask them to tell you how they did the unexpected and went on with their lives and overcame the disaster. Share these recollections with your kids when they are experiencing events that feel similarly devastating. Time and past experience can help us to survive, but it is always easier to learn from the wisdom of others than from personal pain.

NEW LIFE

Becoming a parent is like taking a trip to a foreign country: You have no way of knowing beforehand what you'll encounter once you get there.

—ANN DOUGLAS

• • • •

When you bring home your first child, it can be terrifying to realize you have responsibility for a new life. The problem is that when we are terrified and focus on the fears gnawing away at us, we start thinking only about how we can change things in order to stop the fear and unrest. What some of us end up doing is distracting or numbing ourselves, which accomplishes nothing and finds no real solution.

We need to focus, not on the fact that we are mere incomplete mortals, but on the fact that we are capable of loving this amazing creation who has the potential to change the world. When you do what comes naturally, you are more likely to do it right. When you think of all the parenting books written over the past centuries, you see how the instructions change about things as simple as what to do when your child is crying.

My answer would be to do what your heart tells you to do rather than what some therapist's book tells you is the right way to raise a child. You know my advice is to respond from the heart because we are talking about someone you love.

Talk to people with the same affliction; talk to other parents and get their advice about what works and doesn't work. Your child is a survivor and will eventually educate you and help you to become a better parent. So why be terrified when you have just been given the gift of a wise soul who can guide you to a place of peace, love, and healing?

> **HOW TO MAKE THE MAGIC:** Have several children so you can enjoy them free of the fear and problems encountered with the first one! And as Henny Youngman said, "If you have many children your spouse may get lost in the crowd."

TOUGH DECISIONS

When making a decision of minor importance, I have always found it advantageous to consider all the pros and cons. In vital matters, however, such as the choice of a mate or a profession, the decision should come from the unconscious, from somewhere within ourselves. In the important decisions of personal life, we should be governed, I think, by the deep inner needs of our nature.

—SIGMUND FREUD

• • • •

Shortly after my parents were married, my father lost his job. My mother's parents were not too thrilled with her choice of a husband, and the job loss would only confirm their opinion, so my father would dress every morning as if he were going to work and spend the day at the unemployment office.

One day the phone rang and my father said to my mother, "Rose, I have two job offers. One is a civil service job, which is secure but you don't go anywhere. The other is with Paramount Pictures. It is insecure, but I could go somewhere. Which should I take?"

What would you answer? There is only one answer when difficult, complex, or simple decisions are to be made. Whether someone is asking you what you want for dinner, if you want to go to a movie, whether they should undergo chemotherapy, or what job to take, the only correct answer is "Do what will make you happy." That is what my mother answered and my father did.

These choices are never about the end result. They're not about what will get you more money or a longer life but what is the correct choice and what feels right for you. Happiness does not come from thinking about what is right for you; it comes from feeling what is right. Being a success doesn't make you happy, but being happy makes you a success. So, when your children are torn between two major decisions in their lives, avoid lecturing or imposing your own perspective or opinion. Instead, tell them that they should do what makes them happy, and that will make you happy as well. Through your support and your love, they will learn to make the right decisions for themselves.

HOW TO MAKE THE MAGIC: Practice giving yourself and your family choices, and teach them to focus on feelings as the decision maker. Focus on your own, too. From what college to attend or what job to take, or even what to have for dinner or what to do for fun tonight, get your heart involved. It knows the way to happiness.

GIVE NOTICE BEFORE
BIG CHANGES

The future has a way of arriving unannounced.

—GEORGE WILL

* * * *

Moving your home from one community to another can be hard on everyone, especially the kids. They aren't the ones making the decision, and they often have no say at all. Sometimes they don't even know a move may be in the works until it is a done deal. Most parents who decide to move or take a new job are far more likely to simply announce what is about to happen than to ask their kids how they feel about such a change. Moving is painful for most kids, particularly when it means changing schools and leaving friends behind. To not even be considered in the decision hurts even more.

My family moved just before my senior year of high school. It was really hard to read-just socially and get to know other students who had grown up together. I don't bother to go back to my high school reunions because I didn't even get to know my classmates. It was very painful for me, so I made a decision to really try to avoid that when my wife and I were raising our own children. When we outgrew our home and had to move to a bigger one, we tried to stay in the same school district so our kids wouldn't have to face such a significant transition. Not all of our kids went to the same school, though, so we had to make a greater effort to ensure that those who were now out of their district could continue in their old schools. One of our sons commuted to junior high school with a neighbor who taught there. Yes, we were fortunate. You can be, too.

According to the great psychologist Carl Jung, our futures are unconsciously prepared long in advance. When you make the effort to find out how your kids feel about impending changes and include their needs in your decisions, you will find solutions to the problems that arise. If you have no choice other than to leave your children's schools behind, be sure to seek extra help, even therapy, for your family while you are adjusting to your new home. Find out if the new schools have any programs for new students. Put out extra effort to help establish your kids in community programs and activities where they can make new friends. And above all, assure them that their feelings matter to you and that you will all work together as a family to adjust to your new situation.

How to Make the Magic: Give your family advance notice when change is brewing. Empower your children by bringing them into the decision-making process in any way you can. No decision is too inconsequential; let your kids help choose what color the house should be or how many floors it should have. Throughout the process, be sure to observe your kids and ask them how they are doing and what they are feeling. Get feedback—and act upon what you learn. And then invite their neighbors and classmates to your house for a party.

GIVE BIRTH TO YOURSELF

Birth is not one act; it is a process.

—ERICH FROMM

• • • •

It has been said that no mother would give birth to her second child if she could truly remember the labor pains of delivering her first. Yet, from what I understand, few mothers actually forget what they endured; they just know that bringing a child into the world is worth the pain it takes to do it. The truth is that labor pains aren't limited to childbirth. Life is filled with the pain of continually giving birth to ourselves. And, like childbirth, when we see it as a process of growth and are accompanied by loved ones, the labor is a lot easier to accept.

We give birth to our children, and they in turn continue to give birth to themselves. They all need independence and separation, and most of them seek that from the time they are old enough to run without help. They need to find their true selves and their unique, chosen way of serving the world. The transitions are sometimes difficult. We all know that kids throw tantrums before kindergarten. Young adults are no different; when making the choice to move away from your family home for the first time, they may choose to be nasty and rude as a way of making the separation feel less painful. If they can make you so angry and frustrated that you're glad to see them go, it's easier for them to leave.

We all want to see our children grow into happy and healthy adults, but how will you feel when they walk out the door and the house is quiet and empty? Nothing will prevent us from missing them, but we can ease the transition for everybody concerned. Be aware of the emotions behind their behavior, no matter how rude it may be or how strongly they insist there's nothing wrong. Remember what it was like for you when you were their age. Share with them what you went through, how you felt, how you got through it, and what you learned from it. And let the experience remind you that you do have your own purpose in life aside from raising your kids.

HOW TO MAKE THE MAGIC: Find a time when the house is quiet and you can enjoy a moment by yourself. If you have a journal, write in it. If you don't have a journal, start one. Write down who you feel you are, not as a wife, husband, mother, or father, but simply as yourself. What would you do with the next six months if you had no children at home? Would you go back to school, change your job, travel, write a book? Keep an ongoing list of all of those things. When your children leave home, whether to kindergarten or to college, get started!

SINGLE PARENTS
NEED SUPPORT

Responsibility is the price of greatness.

—Winston Churchill

. . . .

S ingle parents are not all teenage mothers without jobs or child support, despite the common stereotypes presented in the media. There are many reasons for becoming a single parent—from divorce, desertion, or death of a spouse to an informed choice to go it alone. All single parents face difficulties, one way or another. The problems of an unmarried teen mother with no support are obviously very different from those of a prosperous 35-year-old father whose wife died of cancer, yet both are forced to cope with the emotional, psychological, and financial issues of single parenthood.

Single parents have more in common than they may realize. They alone are responsible for the lives of their children. They alone must help their children become decent human beings capable of giving and receiving love. They alone must encourage their children to dream big and pursue those dreams. They alone must find a way to pay for braces, proms, school trips, soccer equipment, piano lessons, college, and whatever else their kids need to become well-rounded, contributing members of society. And most important, they alone must be both mother and father to their kids.

Single parents have to learn to ask for help. Even if the practical issues of finances, housing, childcare, and education are squared away, family support remains crucial. Grandparents can be a vital asset. They are likely to be loving and accepting of everyone concerned, and they can teach proper parenting techniques. Support groups can also be extremely valuable. People who share the same experience understand as few others can. They are often insightful teachers because they have been there too.

Being a single parent is tough under the best of circumstances. If you are in that situation, please do not hide your wounds. Ask for the support you deserve. And when you feel discouraged or afraid, ask your child to hold you and make you laugh. You'll feel better instantly.

> **How to Make the Magic:** It's easier to take good care of your children when you put yourself in their place. Take time to sit down and write about it. For a moment, act as if you are not the single parent but the child of a single parent. What do you want and need? What would you ask your parent to do for you? When you do this exercise, don't worry about yesterday or tomorrow; just ask yourself how you can give your children the love they need today. Then keep at it, one day at a time. Know that a child who feels loved does not feel deprived.

TALK ABOUT DEATH—
AND SHARE LIFE

If we deny love that is given to us, if we refuse to give love because we fear pain or loss, then our lives will be empty, our loss greater.

—Joseph Addison

• • • •

As horrible as it may seem, there will come a time when you or your children will have to face the death of a family member or friend. Don't be afraid to talk about it. This is particularly important with teenagers, among whom suicide is the third most common cause of death today. Sixty percent of high school students have considered killing themselves, according to a survey conducted by the American Association of Pediatrics. It's not a secret at school, so talk about it with your kids at home. It could save their lives.

When someone commits suicide, they don't just end their own life; they wound everyone who loved them. Many kids blame themselves when a friend or classmate commits suicide. They sometimes feel anxious and depressed, and some may have a tough time getting back to their normal lives. Talking about it can't bring the person back, but it definitely can and will help both you and your kids cope with what has happened.

Sometimes your child will lose a friend or classmate through an accident or illness. At times like that, sharing feelings helps wounded survivors feel less alone and decreases their chances of resorting to self-destructive behavior. Reach out for help if you or your children need it. Find a therapist or grief support group that you are comfortable with.

When one of our children was hospitalized for depression, I used the family sessions to share my own feelings, and I found it very helpful. It's not something to be ashamed of. You do your best as a parent, but sometimes that's not enough to resolve serious problems. That is the nature of life. Therapy and support groups help people process their feelings and learn from the situation so they can go on with life—and help others to heal.

When my father died, what helped me most was visiting heaven in a dream on Father's Day and watching the parade of fathers carrying bright candles. I saw a man whose candle was dark, so I went over to light it. The man turned out to be my father. When I told him I was there to light his candle, he said, "They do light it, but your tears keep putting it out." After that I began living fully again, as I knew he wanted me to.

As parents, our courage has to be even bigger than our children's fears. I know a mother in Toronto whose daughter was resigned to die rather than face a bone marrow transplant following extensive and unsuccessful treatment for cancer. She was exhausted and disheartened and told her mother she didn't want the transplant. Her mother unhooked her from all of her IVs, put her in a wheelchair, wheeled her out of the hospital, and took her for a walk in the snow. They shared their love, the beauty of the night, and the snowflakes falling on their faces. Shifting the focus from the possibility of death to the reality of life convinced the daughter to go through with the cancer treatment. She is alive and well today.

How to Make the Magic: Sit down with your family and talk about their feelings and fears about life and death. Tell them what you would want to say if you had a terminal illness. This is heavy stuff, but it will make living easier—especially if you add a little humor. Then take everyone outside and pretend you are extraterrestrials visiting Earth for the first time, marveling at the beauty of creation.

BE POSITIVE ABOUT HEALING

Parents learn a lot from their children about coping with life.

—Muriel Spark

. . . .

When your children need to undergo something unknown—surgery, perhaps, or any unfamiliar medical procedure—prime them with positive images and expectations of recovery. It's very easy to "hypnotize" them into having a positive experience, because you are their primary authority figure. So speak not from your fear but from your desire to help your child heal. I know from experience how powerful the words of a trusted authority can be for a child.

When our son Keith was four years old, he had a hernia that required surgery. Since I was the most experienced pediatric surgeon available at that time, I felt called upon to do the operation. A week beforehand, I explained everything about the surgery to him and took him to see the hospital rooms he would be in. As a surgeon and a parent, I thought I had done a good job of preparing my son for the experience. After the surgery, I stood right by him in the recovery room. I was there when he opened his eyes and said, "You forgot to tell me it was going to hurt."

That one simple statement broke my heart and reminded me that I was nothing more than a tourist—I had never had surgery, and my son was living the experience.

I ask children to draw pictures of themselves in the operating room so I can get an idea of how they are feeling. I can tell from the drawings which children feel loved and safe and which feel their parents are bringing them to me to be punished. A drawing that uses all of the natural colors, versus one all in black with the child looking like a small insect, tells me a lot. I share these drawings with the parents so they can help their children feel more secure before the surgery ever takes place. You might also want to work with a therapist and guided imagery to change your child's image of what the experience will be like. I have seen dramatic changes in drawings done after a week of this type of therapy. It can redirect your child's fear into confidence. Remember, children who feel loved and safe can survive whatever comes their way.

HOW TO MAKE THE MAGIC: Get a bottle of vitamins and put a new label on it: Rapid Healing Supplement. Make sure your child sees the label and knows what it says, and then give the vitamins to your child before and after the event, along with positive suggestions and images. Record a tape of his favorite stories and songs read and sung by people he loves. Throughout the tape, repeat softly: "My voice will go with you." Have your child draw a picture of himself in the scary situation and talk about what you see. Keep a positive attitude, and he will have the same.

BEHAVE LIKE A SURVIVOR

There are only two ways to live your life. One is as though nothing is a miracle. The other is as though everything is a miracle.

—Albert Einstein

● ● ● ●

I teach survival behavior to people with life-threatening illnesses. There are certain patterns and qualities exhibited by people who exceed a doctor's survival expectations. They include things such as having a sense of meaning in your life, expressing appropriate anger, asking for help, learning to say no to the things you do not want to do, not letting others prescribe what you should do, using painful emotions to change your life rather than make you feel helpless, taking time to play, and living an authentic life. These same qualities, when developed, help make a good parent.

Similar traits can be shown in children with cancer, recovering addicts, or even active military—anyone who is forced to confront his own fallibility and mortality. These are also traits you can help your children to learn. When your children are going through difficult times, these attributes will help them to get through the pain on their own. It may be agonizing to watch them going through this process of self-realization, but it is something we each must do. If you are there to love them, it will hurt much less.

When one of our sons went off to college to help him find himself, I was able to let him go because I had faith in him. When he was younger, it was hard to get him out of the house in the morning. The school kept telling me it was his school phobia, so I took him to a child psychiatrist friend of mine. After a few visits, the psychiatrist called me to tell me to come to his office for a consultation. He smiled and said, "Don't worry about your son—and don't waste your time and money bringing him here."

He told me that when my son came in, he would sit on the couch and stare at him for one hour and never say a word. "That takes courage," my friend said. "Then he does something no one else has ever done. He turns and writes on my velveteen sofa with his finger 'F_ _K YOU' and then turns and says nothing."

My friend chuckled a little at my son's independence. "Don't worry—he'll make it, and if he ever feels the need to see me, let me know."

Our son was dealing with his issues and was able to work through them in his own way. Let your children come to terms with life's lessons on their own, knowing that they always have your love and support.

> **HOW TO MAKE THE MAGIC:** Sit down with your children one at a time and discuss their fears and needs, and also remind them of their strengths. Let them know you have faith in them and that if they ever need help, to just ask. Tell them about survival behavior and that the strongest survivors know they do not have to face it all on their own. Doing these things will help you have faith that when you ask them how they are, they'll be able to answer truthfully.

AGGRESSION WITH A PURPOSE

Love transforms the impulse to fight into the impulse to work or play.

—KARL MENNINGER

• • • •

As a parent, you may find that disagreements are part of daily life. Parents disagree with their children; children disagree with their siblings and friends, and so on. Learning how to deal with disagreements can be a real challenge and a real asset.

When someone disagrees with me or is angry because of something I said, did, or wrote, I always thank them. When they ask why I am thanking them, I tell them that anger is a source of energy, and we can accomplish something with that energy.

An example from my own experience: Let's say a doctor told you that you had six months to live. You could go home, curl up in bed, and die in a week; or you could get angry, tell the doctor a few things he may not want to hear, and then go on and live to prove him wrong.

Show your children how they can utilize their anger for productive and meaningful purposes—and do it with a bit of humor. If your child runs around yelling at his siblings, "I'm going to split your head open," you could suggest to him that he consider becoming a neurosurgeon and get him some anatomy books. If another child loves knocking everyone down, obviously he will be a professional football player someday.

When love is involved, destructive tendencies and aggression can be transformed. Appropriate reactions can be turned into constructive activities. Just don't try to put a lid on anger and aggression issues through criticism and think that will take care of the problem. I am not saying that there shouldn't be rules about appropriate behavior; however, the energy that is within each of us needs to find a productive outlet. So you can hammer away with your anger and put up a building, or end up in jail for destroying property because you have not found a constructive outlet.

HOW TO MAKE THE MAGIC: Get your family together and find out what makes them angry and aggressive, then have them work at finding some constructive ways to direct that energy. Talk about how disagreements and the feelings they bring up can be used in a positive direction, instead of having them lead to separation and pain, these feelings can lead to creativity and healthy competition.

TERRIBLE TWOS
AND OTHER LABELS

For parents, the terrible twos are a psychological preview of puberty. . .
At the age of two or three, children eat only bananas and refuse to get a
haircut. Ten years later, they eat only bananas and refuse to get a haircut.

—Carin Rubenstein

• • • •

Does it really help to label the ages—or stages—kids go through? I think we do it so we won't think that either we have made a terrible mistake or our kids are seriously defective when they suddenly go from being angels to devils overnight. The fact is, these developmental stages tend to happen at certain ages, and they can be extremely trying for parents. Yet many parents have noticed that the stereotypes aren't always on target in terms of age. In a survey conducted by a parenting Web site, more than 80 percent of mothers said that the shrieking tantrums that characterize the "terrible twos" actually occur most frequently toward the end of age two and through most of age three.

Tantrums are exasperating at any age, but like the comedian Jackie Mason said when he was told that he looked horrible after a night of heavy drinking: "You should see it from this side." Kids often have no idea what is making them act so crazy. It might feel even worse to them than it does to us, for all we know. What we have to remember is that their brains are still developing along with the rest of their bodies—and brain development doesn't always keep up with the standard growth charts.

Before you tear your hair out, think about how you deal with a new puppy or kitten. They go through behavioral stages, just like kids do. Puppies go through phases of chewing everything they can find, preferably your favorite shoes or your only briefcase. And kittens may avoid the litter box for reasons it takes weeks to determine: They don't like the smell of this one, the clumps are too big in that one, or there isn't enough privacy without a dome cover. These phases are definitely annoying, but most of us realize that it would be mean and useless to yell at them because they would have no idea what we were so upset about. After all, the puppy was just being a puppy and the kitten was just being a kitten.

Most kids, especially younger ones, react much like puppies and kittens. When you yell at them for a mess they made an hour ago, they go blank. But when we focus on the present moment and talk to our kids about their mistakes—or bad behavior—at the time it is happening, we might have a chance of getting through to them. It's not easy, but it's not hopeless, either. Look how many people have lived through raising kids!

HOW TO MAKE THE MAGIC: When you think you cannot live with your child's behavior for one more minute, pretend you have come in to consult with me about the intolerable situation. I tell you a version of an old wise proverb: I can avoid drug therapy for your child if you get me a white hair from the chest of a bear. You spend months befriending a wild bear in order to get that single strand of hair. You return to my office, hand me the precious hair, and I immediately toss it into the fireplace. When you finish screaming at me, I give you the advice you have needed all along: "Now go home and be as patient with your child as you were with the bear."

DEALING WITH PREJUDICE

*We are each burdened with prejudice—against the poor or the rich,
the smart or the slow, the gaunt or the obese. It is natural to
develop prejudices. It is noble to rise above them.*

—AUTHOR UNKNOWN

• • • •

What do you do when you move into a new neighborhood and your child is called names at school and bullied for being a certain race or religion? Even worse, what do you do when someone paints graffiti on your garage door or makes unsettling statements to threaten you?

First you must protect your children and let them know that they are not the problem, and there are a lot of people in the world who need help and don't always act in a loving and intelligent way. The Anti-Defamation League has advice for families, so report the event to them and seek their help. Respond to your children and let them know their feelings are not to be judged. Fear and sadness are okay. Tell them that you want to know whatever happens and that they shouldn't hide anything out of fear that their parents will do something crazy and make things worse. Commend them for having the courage to stand up for what is right. Together with your children, come up with a plan of action, which will include meeting with school officials, local clergy, support groups, witnesses, and the perpetrators and their parents.

By taking affirmative action, you will help your community come together to support you and show those responsible they are the minority. I can recall, when attending college, being left out of fraternities and events because of my religion. I wonder what would have happened if I had simply spoken up? Today the school is completely different; it's respectful of diversity, with many races and religions having their own study centers and courses.

How to Make the Magic: Speak out against anyone who targets people or groups with slanderous humor or illegal actions. Don't be a bystander. Stand up for those targeted, and educate yourself about other religions and races so you can educate your family and others and be supportive of those who are different. Find those who agree with your point of view and work together. Imagine the kind of role model you'll be for your kids.

CHOOSE PEACE OR CONFLICT

Better than a thousand hollow words, is one word that brings peace.

—BUDDHA

. . . .

One evening, our five children were driving me nuts because they were fighting at the dinner table, so I stood up and said, "You may choose peace or you may choose conflict!" Our daughter answered, "I'll choose pizza." The laughter ended the problem.

The truth is we are here for a limited amount of time, and we should think about how to spend this lifetime. I prefer peace and, therefore, do not bother myself with disruptive events or people who cause problems for me. I solve the problem as calmly as I can and move on. Whether a situation is bordering on catastrophic, such as a robbery or a broken furnace in the middle of winter, or trivial, such as an argument between our children about who is better at a certain video game, issues should be dealt with in a clearheaded and peaceable manner. Creating more conflict merely makes the incident much more chaotic and difficult for everyone.

Starting arguments, blaming others, or internalizing anger is not the way to go through life. Treat the problem knowing that you will get through it, and you will be a better person because of it. Remember, you can spend your life being angry or joyful. You control only one thing: your thoughts. So find the serenity within yourself. Or as my wife says, "Never go to bed mad. Stay up and fight." Keep your sense of humor, express your feelings, and recognize your power, and you will spend more time at peace than at war. Some nights, a nice pizza will help you find peace, too.

> **HOW TO MAKE THE MAGIC:** Discuss the value of peace of mind versus conflict with the family. Remind them that you are not denying their needs and right to express themselves; instead, the issue is about how a problem is approached. Perhaps you can create an arbitration board from family members and rotate who is on the board so that problems can be listened to and solved. When everyone listens, they are able to understand each other's perspective—and that's the solution.

LOVE, MAGIC & MUDPIES

TIME TO LISTEN

Make a memory with your children, Spend some time to show you care;
Toys and trinkets can't replace those precious moments that you share.
Money doesn't buy real pleasure, it doesn't matter where you live;
Children need your own attention, something only you can give.
Childhood's days pass all too quickly, happy memories all too few;
Plan to do that special something, take the time to go or do.
Make a memory with your children, take the time in busy days;
Have some fun while they are growing, show your love in gentle ways.

—ELAINE HARDT

• • • •

How can we truly get to know one another? We can do it by listening to each other, but the problem is that families rarely make time or feel they have the time to listen to each other. We are all busy doing, running, and scheduling, and who has time for talking?

How often do we mean it when we ask our kids and spouse, "How was your day?"

What we expect is the usual "Okay." Then off we go to do our mechanical and often meaningless things, which do need to get done but could also wait a few minutes while we listen to each other speak from our hearts. How can we create a successful family that is focused upon all of its members and not the self-interest of individuals?

What we need to do is have a family hour that doesn't even have to last an hour but begins at a certain time. It can be before dinner, at bedtime—whatever suits the family is fine. With a family of seven, like ours, each evening one member has charge of the talking hour. You can be flexible scheduling these sessions depending upon your family makeup.

Give each person in the family a time to talk about what is going on with them and what they are experiencing in their lives. Everyone is to listen and not interrupt or ask questions. When the speaker is done, then you as a parent are to step in with the following exercise.

HOW TO MAKE THE MAGIC: When the session is done, ask everyone what they learned from listening with an open mind and heart. Ask each member how they felt on a personal level and how they feel it may relate to the family. Their responses are not to contain critical comments but instead should relate to personal reactions and feelings. Keep the lines of communication open, and make sure you make the time to listen . . . from the heart.

GIVE THEM SOME SPACE

*Stop trying to perfect your child, but keep trying to perfect
your relationship with him.*

—DR. HENKER

. . . .

Don't feel guilty about sending your kids away once in a while. Summer camps or boarding schools can help them and you. When one of our sons was having problems, we enrolled him in a residential school where he could receive therapy and an excellent education. The separation was good for all of us. When he came home for the weekend, we enjoyed spending time together rather than hounding him about doing his homework or arguing about other problems. We were able to be loving parents when together rather than only his disciplinarians. We all were relieved and able to enjoy our time together and our new roles.

This same son also loved to spend time at his grandparents' house. He would often tell us at the dinner table, "Grandma called. She wants me to come and visit her." We'd take him to the bus Friday evening, and off he'd go for a weekend adventure with Grandma and Grandpa. Years later, when our son was an adult, he told us that he had lied about his grandma calling. He had been the one who initiated the whole thing. The truth was that whenever he felt he just wanted to get away, he would phone his grandma and tell her he was coming to visit.

The moral of this story is that kids need time away from their parents as much as parents need time away from their kids. It's a natural fact of life and nothing to feel guilty or ashamed about. I'm glad that our son got to spend time with his grandparents and got a little R & R at the same time.

HOW TO MAKE THE MAGIC: Let your kids experience a change of scenery now and then. It doesn't matter whether they visit family or close friends, go to summer camp, or attend a residential school. What's important is letting them get away so both of you can periodically experience a different atmosphere. They will experience your faith and trust in them and learn to make decisions they can rely upon. They will also have things to share with you that are unique experiences for them, thus enhancing their growth while increasing their self-esteem.

GETTING THROUGH DIVORCE

It is easier to build strong children than to repair broken men.

—FREDERICK DOUGLAS

* * * *

I often share with parents one of the punch lines I used when our five kids were getting out of hand: "Do you know why your mother and I will never get a divorce?"

They would say, "Why not, Dad?"

And I would jokingly answer, "Because neither one of us wants the children."

That response may seem humorous when parents are getting along, and the children understand the statement is your symbolic message to cool it, but it isn't funny when divorce is a real possibility. The greatest challenge in a marriage is realizing it is a relationship and not just about the needs of the individuals involved to the exclusion of the needs of others. A family is a community, and all parts of the community must be cared for just like the parts of your body. You cannot focus on one part to the exclusion of the others and expect a human body, or a marriage, to remain healthy. The problems that accompany divorce, which also affect all the members of the family, are guilt, shame, and blame. Whose fault is it when there is a divorce? When one person is self-destructive, everyone knows where the blame lies. But when a family just falls apart, who carries the burden of guilt? This is an issue that must be faced and discussed, and many may need a trained counselor to help them.

Parents often vent their anger at the children while going through the tough times around divorce. This can cause the children to internally feel they are to blame for the problems in the marriage. Their assumption is that if they had only been better children, Mom and Dad would not be splitting up. I can recall a patient of mine, who had cancer, saying, "My parents committed suicide, so I must have been a failure as a child." She spent her life, until she developed cancer, afraid of relationships because of her belief.

It is important for parents to let children know the real issues and, depending on their age, that the children receive an explanation of the reasons for the divorce or separation. The real facts will free them from this burden of guilt. As part of the explanation, let them know they are loved and are not the problem or the reason for the divorce. Also give them the freedom to share their feelings, whether healthy or unhealthy, loving or critical.

How to Make the Magic: The walls have ears and so do your children. When divorce becomes a real possibility, set up a family session to discuss it, and leave plenty of time so that the session will not be rushed. Give everyone the opportunity to say what they feel, and tell the children to speak from their hearts and not be afraid to share their thoughts and emotions. Who knows, after a few sessions like this, you may even change your mind about getting a divorce. We are all wounded, and the wounds need to be shared if we are to heal our lives and bodies.

WHEN YOUR CHILD IS SICK OR INJURED

There will always be some curveballs in your life.
Teach your children to thrive in that adversity.

—Jeanne Moutoussamy-Ashe

• • • •

I am not talking here about some cold or minor injury that creates temporary lifestyle changes in your child's life, but about significant and even life-threatening problems. First, let go of the guilt that all parents feel for not making the diagnosis sooner or for letting them go on some trip where the accident occurred. The past is over, and dwelling upon it is of no help to anyone. Forgive everyone involved and move on.

Obviously, you want to seek the best medical help available. Do not accept what a health professional tells you without getting a second opinion from a specialist or a major medical center where the problem is treated frequently. Do not be afraid to speak up as a parent so they know you and your child.

Help your child to feel empowered by including him or her in the decision-making process. Obviously, age plays a role, but simple things like asking which arm they prefer blood to be drawn from, or whether they want to walk or sit in a wheelchair, can make them part of the process. If they are hospitalized, be sure to provide them with a water gun or squirt toy to use on anyone who does not respect them. Also leave paper and crayons by the bed so you can analyze their feelings by the colors they use and the things they draw. When you want specific information, ask them to draw themselves and their treatment and their doctor, as an example.

Do not live in a fearful future, as it disrupts the ability to heal. Live in the moment as children instinctively do. A pediatric surgeon who studied kids with cancer found that adults with chronic illnesses don't stay in the moment. Kids do. They are interested in the pleasure of the moment, so learn from them. The past is history, the future a mystery, so enjoy the moment. That's why it is called the present.

Children, like animals, have a sense of wholeness even when parts of their bodies are not functioning. They identify with who they are and not what is missing or dysfunctional. Learn from them and don't label them by an affliction or missing part or ability. I know many children with chronic diseases who are changing the world they live in because of their diseases. So the disability can make them beautiful and bring meaning into their lives and become a blessing. I remember the courage of Sue Ann, who had athetoid cerebral palsy. To type her autobiography, she had to be tied to a chair and gagged, so she wouldn't drool on the computer keys, and then she typed more than two hundred pages with her nose. The title of her book: *The Bird with the Broken Wing.*

Last but not least, learn to be there. Studies have shown that you can help heal your child just with your presence.

HOW TO MAKE THE MAGIC: If your child or someone in your family is living with an illness or disability, be with them and ask them how they feel, how you can help, and what is on their mind. Then listen for as long as they need to talk. You do not need to have a solution. They will find their own. They will hear themselves say what they need while you listen.

PART SEVEN

THE SOUL IN PARENTING

Do not live your life as if every day were going to be your last, but live it as if it were going to be the last day for those you love.

—Anonymous

• • • •

I often say that the three biggest problems any child has are his parents, teachers, and religion. I had loving parents, did very well in school, and felt comfortable with my Creator. However, quite often, these three authority groups are telling children how to live by offering teachings that require a rigid lifestyle; they supply the words kids must live by, or suffer punishment in this life and ever after.

For me, in contrast to more authoritarian approaches to finding the way, the key is spirituality. An atheist can be spiritual, too. Spirituality is free of the rules and regulations imposed by others, and yet truly spiritual teachings help us to find a path that leads toward a meaningful, thriving, and soulful life. Many religions have a primitive history and war gods, and many teachings inspire battles over differences and beliefs. Spirituality should unite all living things because it recognizes that we are all made of the same thing, come from the same place, and will ultimately return to our source. As Thornton Wilder wrote, "All those impulses of love return to the love that made them." Put simply, the Dalai Lama describes his religion as kindness to all things.

When your children grow up with a solid spiritual base that teaches them to be kind to all living things, they will be free to be in touch with their souls. When they are taught kindness, acceptance, and love, they will have open minds and hearts; they'll be able to observe the effects of prayer and consciousness upon life and well-being. Many studies show the health benefits of belonging to a congregation and attending religious services; this connection can be a resource to sustain children. We must use religion just as we do mythology: to teach us to get to the soul of parenting; to see all the world's children as children of God; and to know that we've all been given life to manifest God's will, which is to love thy neighbor and not do unto others that which you would not want done unto you or your loved ones. When we are raised as soulful children, the voice we listen to will be the voice of the Creator and not just the material world.

IT'S MAGIC

We are here to experience life and not to explain it.

—Bernie Siegel

• • • •

Without love there can be no magic. Love helps you to see the uniqueness and beauty in every child. Even unwanted children carry their own magic into the world. Whether we are creating a child or healing a wound, something very magical happens in those moments. An inner intelligence seeks to maintain life and does not need our directions. Remember that your state of mind speaks to this creative force through your feelings and biology, and it makes a difference. As a friend who was confronting a life-threatening illness said, "When you live in your heart, magic happens." When you help your family open their eyes to the wonder of it all, they too will become aware of the magic. I know that parenting and family life can be very difficult at times, but when you focus on the miracle of creation, keep love in your heart, and do not live in fear, you can enjoy the opportunity to be a parent and the blessings that come with such a huge job. Keep hope alive and let the magic thrive.

How to Make the Magic: Take your children on nature walks, on bird- and whale-watching trips, or to museums and aquariums. Spend some time watching sunrises or sunsets on the beach. Visit a zoo and talk about how the animals live together, how they communicate, how they share and help and take care of their own kids. Think of as many ways as you can to share the wonder and magic of life with your children. And do not be afraid to discuss the unexplained wonders of creation, quantum physics, astronomy, and more. Evolution and intelligent design are both a part of life. As Ruth Gordon said in the movie *Harold and Maude:* "I don't pray; I communicate with life."

UNDERSTANDING
AND FORGIVENESS

We may not know how to forgive, and we may not want to forgive; but the very fact we say we are willing to forgive begins the healing practice.

—LOUISE HAY

• • • •

I cannot help thinking that animals and children are the greatest teachers about understanding and forgiveness. They do not hold on to thoughts about the past or worry about what is truly meaningless, as we adults do. I watch them accidentally hurt each other or break a toy and get into conflict over it, and yet a few hours later they are playing together and enjoying each other's company.

They understand what I call survival behavior. Survivors don't whine and make excuses; they live in the moment and move on so past events do not affect their entire lives and relationships and continue to deprive them of a joyful life. They can laugh at the past and the lessons learned from it. I know that for me, just trying to forget a slight never really works. I remain trapped by that experience. My attempts to tuck it away someplace where I will not be aware of it or reminded of it just do not work. I have learned that those experiences keep coming back, both consciously and unconsciously, to haunt me and affect my life.

When I am able to forgive, or even work on the process of forgiveness, I find a big shift in my thinking and peace of mind. Admittedly, forgiveness does take work. I admire those saints who are capable of forgiving without understanding the reason something happened or why someone acted as they did. For me, the road to forgiveness has to begin with understanding both the people involved and the actions for which I want to forgive them. I also reflect on the fact that trying to forget never really gets me what I need; but when I can forgive, I give myself the gift of freedom from a burden I do not want to carry.

Conversely, if there are things you have done that you wish you hadn't, and you are trying to forget them, reverse the process. Explain to those involved why you did what you did and what you have learned, and then finish with an apology. If they can't forgive you, that is their problem and no longer yours to carry. You must learn to forgive yourself.

For the health of your soul and that of your family, embrace forgiveness. Doing so will help you maintain your family's integrity; everyone will feel safe, loved, and understood, no matter what events the future presents them with. When your family feels this unconditional security, you have created an environment where understanding and forgiveness can blossom.

How to Make the Magic: Think about family events or interactions that you wish you could forget. Now go to the family members involved and ask them if they would talk with you about them. This process is especially vital for parents and their adult children. Young children let you know the reasons they feel hurt or hurt you, while older and adult children are busy denying feelings and events that hurt them. Clarify that this conversation will not be about blame or guilt but about a need to understand, forgive, and move on to a place where love can once again exist in your relationship.

A WORLD FAMILY

*Our greatest strength lies not in how much we differ from each other
but in how much—how very much—we are the same.*

—Eknath Easwaran

. . . .

Think for a moment about your goals for your family. Do you want your family to be the best family in the world or the best family *for* the world? Those are two very different concepts.

If you focus your family on self-interest, material things, or impressing the neighbors with your abilities, finances, green lawn, or clean house, you may be referred to as the best in the world, but what have you done for the world? When you are for the world, you are a creator, and your every act takes into consideration how your neighbors are affected. (And by neighbors, I mean all those who inhabit our planet.)

When you are for the world, material things are used to help the world. Recycling becomes a way of life. Rescuing others and supporting charitable acts all become family events. The focus is on how to make the world a better place, not just how to make your family's life better or get a bigger house or a pool in the backyard.

When you are the best family for the world, you are thinking about how future generations will live on this planet. Remember, we are talking about your family's future generations, too!

HOW TO MAKE THE MAGIC: Sit down and review what you and your family do to make all of you the best family for the world. Consider revising the list and refocusing it so that it includes making choices to support what your neighbors and future generations need from you, too. Then start doing those things now. Even the smallest acts can make a difference.

GET AWAY FROM IT ALL

The best remedy for those who are afraid, lonely, or unhappy is to go outside, somewhere where they can be quiet, alone with the heavens, nature, and God. Because only then does one feel that all is as it should be and that God wishes to see people happy, amidst the simple beauty of nature.

—ANNE FRANK

. . . .

How about getting away from it all with the family? I mean that literally. Leave all the electronic gear at home and go camp out in the woods somewhere, or rent a cabin off-season in the middle of nowhere, if you are not into camping. I can recall lying on the floor of a cabin with a bunch of Cub Scouts, one of whom was our son, and listening to the things they talked about when they thought I was asleep. It was very hard to keep from laughing.

Get the gang out there and share a confined space within the vast openness of nature. More important, share what is on your mind when you are unable to distract yourselves with cell phones, electronic gadgets, and loud noises. I want you to know the loudest noise you will ever hear is silence. If you can't stay overnight, take a long hike or climb a mountain. When there are no distractions, you will become very aware of the inner voice, which keeps speaking to you all the time. We rarely pay attention because we are so busy doing instead of being.

> **HOW TO MAKE THE MAGIC:** Start looking into available sites where you can take your family to get away from it all. Look for places both close to home and far away, places where you can be together and share the voice of nature while also listening to each other's inner wisdom. While out in nature, observe the trees, streams, creatures, and the nature of life. Listen for your children's words of wisdom to you. When you get home, you will be surprised by how many people didn't even know you were away.

THE DIVINE

*We spin around the Sun with six billion of us and somehow through
divine providence we landed right here right now.*

—Byron Dorgan

. . . .

While I was writing this book, I found a quote of something I apparently said many years ago. Reading the quote was very therapeutic because at the time I was feeling a bit overwhelmed. "To experience love—that is the sum total of the whole reason for the existence of the universe." As a parent, it is so easy to lose touch with the Divine in daily life.

I believe in the message of this quote, for many reasons. As a physician, I have seen so-called incurable diseases disappear when people changed their lives and chose to simply love, leave their troubles to God, or make the world beautiful before they died. We are all part of the great plan and originate out of the divine stuff that created it all. Just think of something as simple as a wound healing, and you realize the wisdom within each of us.

Now if this is all true, why is it so hard to remember? To me, the answer is simple: We have too much to think about—credit cards, jobs, schedules, friends, families, responsibilities. We also have to be aware that when we are not loving and in touch with the Divine, when we are living in fear under stressful conditions, we become more vulnerable to disease.

Look for the Divine in your daily life, see it in your children, your loved ones, and your world, and notice how much love you feel when you do.

> **HOW TO MAKE THE MAGIC:** Write "To experience love is the reason for the existence of the universe" and put it up in the kitchen and every bathroom in the house. And make darn sure that you take it to heart, demonstrate that you mean it, and help your family to live the message, too. When you live the message, you will be doing your job as a parent: to bring heaven down to earth.

SOUL, SPIRIT, AND ANGELS

What can you ever really know of other people's souls—of their temptations, their opportunities, their struggles? One soul in the whole creation you do know, and it is the only one whose fate is placed in your hands.

—C. S. LEWIS

. . . .

Let me go way out there for a moment and share some of the things that make life an interesting mystery. One question might be: Do we select our parents? Is it possible that our consciousness selects whom our parents will be based upon our past life experience and what we need to teach and learn in this life? A bit mind-blowing to even consider it, but who knows? My wife would answer, "God only knows."

Could there be energy around us, that some would call spirit and others angels, which is here to guide us and help us experience what we are here for and sustain us through difficult experiences? Frankly, I do not know and simply keep my mind open to possibilities, just as the astronomers and quantum physicists do.

But if we do select our parents, then you have a very important job to perform. You can be the spirit and soul who provides your child with the support he or she needs to thrive. Be there whenever they need to be lifted on your wings above the strife. It is the absence of love and compassion that causes so many problems with children. When you supply these essential feelings, you are literally an angel for your child.

Your child's soul must flourish and grow, just as yours must to live a soulful life. That is what we are all here to do. This is not about who, what, or why we were created but about living the experience in a meaningful way. When parents find meaning and live a life of spirit, they can pass it on via their psychological genes to their children.

I always feel I must repeat that this is not about religion, words, guilt, shame, and blame but about living a life that enhances all forms of life on this planet. It's tragic that some religions lead to war and not to love. Anything that leads to destruction is not an appropriate component of parenting.

HOW TO MAKE THE MAGIC: Remember the old saying "Make love and not war." As my bumper sticker says, "When the power of love overcomes the love of power, the world will know peace." May it be someday because of your children.

TRUST AND FAITH

Begin to weave and God will provide the thread.

—GERMAN PROVERB

. . . .

For me, trust and faith very much go together. When I know I can trust another person, I have faith in that person because I know how he or she will act or react in any given situation. I can rely on this person to be there for me in a predictable way. That may include disagreeing with me, too.

Show your children that you can be someone in whom they can have faith. Show them you are someone they can trust to attend their baseball games, applaud them at their ballet recitals, and pick them up after school. If children are able to trust their parents, they are more likely to develop healthy relationships with others when they are older. It also helps them to know that you love and support them through everything.

One of our children is quite depressed, as I write this, because of a variety of health problems that are causing him pain and limiting his life. Trying to help him is not an easy thing to do when all he talks about is how awful he feels and how living is of questionable value, and he won't listen to what I have to offer. In the midst of all this, knowing how hard it is for me to listen to him talk about his pain while he won't really listen to me, he said, "But I need you to still love me."

He knows he can rely on that. He can trust me when I say yes, I will always love you, and he can have faith that I will live up to my words and show up tomorrow to listen and offer my love and any help I can. His trust and faith are not in my ability to cure every affliction but to be there and share the experience, whatever it may be. Fortunately, there are joyful moments, too, and I try to help him to have faith that he will find those moments again in the future.

How to Make the Magic: Have your family act out the trust game. One person stands behind the other and asks, "Do you trust me?" Next, the other person says "yes" and falls backwards and is caught in the first person's arms. This classic game can help everyone to see that they can trust each other to be there for them.

THE MAGIC OF LIFE

For magic to happen in your life, you must believe in magic.

—Grandmother, quoted by Lynn Andrews

• • • •

As we guide our children through life, we need to remember not to focus so much on reason and rationality that we block out the indescribable feeling of awe we should be sharing with our children. Who can explain the origin of the universe? How does a wound heal? Why does ice defy the laws of physics and float? How does a seed know which way is up? Why do the leaves turn color in the fall? How is a child created from one cell?

I remember our son Jonathan having an invisible friend when he was a youngster. We never discouraged him from having this invisible companion, who apparently was responsible for many acts Jon carried out that his parents didn't approve of. I hear from so many health professionals about their intuitive and spiritual insights as youngsters that were considered bizarre and not to be discussed by their parents.

I suggest you give your children a life filled with M&Ms—mystery and mastery—so the doorway to life opens before them. Magic is another M that will come to them if you give them the freedom to explore possibilities. Just because you can't explain or understand something does not mean it didn't happen or doesn't exist. Keep your world, and that of your child, open to all possibilities.

> **HOW TO MAKE THE MAGIC:** Teach your children to become open and aware of the mystery and magic of life and to accept what they experience. Let them know everything doesn't have to be explained to be experienced and accepted. Take them to a planetarium, get them a telescope and microscope, visit interesting museums, and expose them to the magic of life. Help them become masters of their own existence.

RAISE CONSCIOUS CHILDREN

Children are the living messages
we send to a time we will not see.

—John W. Whitehead

. . . .

Are your children conscious or unconscious? When I talk about unconscious children, I don't mean those who actually are in a coma but those who act as if they are. They are unaware of—and care little about—how their actions and words might affect others.

It's easy to assume that these self-centered kids are simply ill-natured, but that's not necessarily true. Many of them have unwittingly enclosed themselves in an "it's all about me" cocoon so they can hide from their uncomfortable feelings. Suppose a boy's alcoholic mother abandoned him on his grandma's doorstep, and he comforted himself by eating sweets all day until he was seriously overweight. At home he might seem quiet and maybe a little depressed, but at school he could be an arrogant bully. It's easy to see how being a bully would cover up overwhelming feelings of fear and inadequacy. Wounded people often hide from emotions, which renders them unconscious to the feelings and needs of people around them as well.

You can help your children to become conscious by acting that way yourself. They grow up imitating you, so when you perform small acts of kindness—and don't forget yourself!—they will follow suit. You don't need to spend thousands of dollars on special therapies, camps, and counselors. Just let them see you offering apologies, opening doors for others, assisting the disabled, helping other shoppers at the supermarket, raking your neighbor's leaves, shoveling snow for your grandparents, and so forth. Invite them to participate. Notice when they initiate acts of kindness on their own, and praise them for it. One of the best ways children can learn to be conscious is to be around animals. Our children grew up surrounded by various species. They learned about each animal's needs and how to be conscious of those needs. It made for some interesting experiences for me, too. There were times I came home to find goats and guinea pigs in prolonged, painful labor and had to get back into my physician mode so I could be their obstetrician.

Having animals also helped our children to become conscious of the fact that death is a reality and we can't save everyone we love. Mostly the experience of loss taught them to be conscious of life and how important it is to make it as easy as possible for others. Are any of us perfect in this area? No, but we are conscious of our imperfections and do not let them create more pain in the world.

HOW TO MAKE THE MAGIC: Arrange for your kids to volunteer at a local assisted living facility. Talking with seniors and disabled residents will teach them a lot about what is important in life—and will expand their consciousness. Or have them volunteer at an animal shelter or other place where they can share kindness and clearly see the needs of others and, at least for a short while, put those needs above their own.

HOW TO SAVE THE WORLD

No act of kindness, however small, is ever wasted.

—AESOP

. . . .

S top and think about what you are teaching your child about being charitable. Are you helping him to make the world a better place, rather than encouraging him to think only about his personal comforts? I saw a short film about a child in the United States who learned of the lack of water in Africa and started raising funds to dig wells there. Through his efforts, he raised hundreds of thousands of dollars. He went to Africa and visited the village and people whom he had helped to survive by providing them with clean water to drink. Imagine how proud his parents were!

Even on a smaller level, you can encourage your kids to reach out and help. Read the papers each day and see who is in need. An animal hit by a car needs his vet bills paid. You can help. Someone's home burns down. You can help. When our rabbit, Smudge, died, we built a rabbit rescue facility at our local shelter called Smudge's Place. It made me feel better to know something good had come out of our loss. You can do the same thing with the losses your family experiences; teaching your kids to turn a tragedy into something positive is a tremendous life skill, and one that will ultimately leave the world a far better place. Remember that blessings are the events that help you and your children to become more complete human beings, and that sometimes what turns out to be a blessing might not feel very good when it first happens. Help your children to focus on what they can do, rather than what they can't do, to save the world. Change happens one step at a time; that's how miracles get started.

HOW TO MAKE THE MAGIC: Get the family together and decide on which charities or causes you want to support with your time, money, and energy. Then make a plan and go do it. There is no wrong decision or cause when you are helping others.

HELP THEM FOLLOW
THEIR BLISS

*Go confidently in the direction of your dreams! Live the life you've
imagined. As you simplify your life, the laws of the universe will be simpler.*

—Henry David Thoreau

• • • •

As parents, we want our children to listen to their hearts, discover their gifts and talents, and follow the path that leads them toward happiness and fulfillment. Sometimes a child will display an exceptional ability in an area that you find surprising. His talent could be related to consciousness from a past life that he brought with him when he was born. That may sound like way-out mystical stuff to you, but I actually have experienced two events that made me a believer, one as a child and one as an adult.

When I was four years old, I almost choked to death on a toy I had swallowed, and I had an out-of-body experience. I left my body yet could see myself on the bed, choking.

I never stopped to think about how I could still see, even though I was near death. That is, until later in my life, when I read about people born blind who had near death experiences and could also see when they left their bodies. Many were very upset when they were resuscitated, back in their bodies, and still blind. To me this type of experience says that consciousness is separate from our bodies. I believe that when we are born, we bring with us a portion of this consciousness. This helps me to understand how and why, as an adult, I went into a trance and experienced a past life after a friend asked over the phone, "Why are you living this life?" What I experienced was myself, as a knight, following orders and killing with a sword. I won't go into the gory details, which left me sobbing, but my first reaction to my friend was, "Maybe that's why I became a surgeon, to heal with a knife and not kill." My experiences gave me many questions about consciousness and how and why we are living this life. They opened my mind past the point of what I thought I believed and allowed me to see life from a broader perspective.

What does this have to do with being a good parent? It is a reminder that the most important thing we give our children is the freedom to live the life they have come here to live, rather than pushing them to live a life we think they should want. And the only way we can get a glimpse of what they came here to do is to watch carefully for signs of their special interests or talents. I have wondered about many of my own strong interests: my profession as a surgeon, my preoccupation with rescuing animals, my choice to have a large family, and my volunteer efforts to help other people. What made me want all of these things? Perhaps, if I used a sword in a past life to kill people and animals, then in this life I could be atoning for that by rescuing, volunteering, and using a knife to cure people and animals.

HOW TO MAKE THE MAGIC: I see our consciousness as similar to a compact disc. Once a track is recorded on a CD, it is always there, whether you listen to it or not, like the consciousness we carry within us. When each of us is born, we have a unique CD within us. It plays itself out over our lifetime; we hear our own song and others hear theirs. Our job as parents is to encourage our children to listen to their own songs and sing them joyfully, exactly as they hear them.

PART EIGHT

PARENTS NEED CARE, TOO

I will never forget when, almost thirty years ago, I was an angry, tired husband and father. To learn how to survive as a parent and physician, I attended a weeklong seminar run by Elisabeth Kübler-Ross. She was counseling people who were confronting serious illness, and she had written a book on death and dying and the stages of anger, depression, denial, bargaining, and acceptance involved. She said to me, "You have needs, too."

As parents, we must all become conscious of those words and their message. We must remember that our children's needs are important, but so are our own; and we must not be guided by what makes us feel guilty, but instead by what makes us feel happy. You cannot stay healthy and care for your family if you do not take care of yourself.

Regular exercise, proper nutrition, taking time for yourself, and self-expression are extremely important for parents to thrive and survive. You can live and demonstrate the message you want your children to be aware of, and live well also. I like to jog, but instead of doing it after I came home from a day's work, I would get up early in the morning to go out and run. In that way I could take care of myself and have time for my family, too. It is an individual choice when you decide to take the needed time for yourself, and not something to get angry about because you have to get up early to do it.

If you constantly say yes to everyone else's needs in the family, you are saying no to yourself and at some point will get sick in order to get time off. Remember, you don't need sick days; you need health days. Give yourself the same priority as you do your child when you are deciding what is best for you and your own needs.

A PERFECT WORLD

When we love our children more than we hate our enemies,
wars will cease.

—Golda Meir

• • • •

When your children see disturbing images of mothers and children being killed in a war, they may ask you why God let that happen. What is your answer? You can say that people, not God, wage wars. And you can say that we do not live in a perfect world. "But," they may ask, "why didn't God create a perfect world for us? Why didn't he give us a world without war, hunger, illness, or hate?"

To seek an answer to that question, I am going to ask you to put yourself in God's place for a day. What would you do? Most people say they would stop wars and put an end to all of the problems they read about every day in the newspaper. Yet God did not choose to do that. The reason he gave me (the last time I consulted him) is that what we see as a perfect world would be a magic trick, not a real creation. If there were no problems of any kind, all of our acts of kindness, compassion, and love would be utterly meaningless. Would that be truly perfect? Not really.

When you explain that to your kids, be sure to also tell them that each of us gets to choose how we will respond to the cries of the world. When we answer with loving-kindness, we make the world a more perfect place. That's how God lets us participate in creation. Everything we do changes the world, bit by bit. Make sure your children know that everything they do to help does make a difference.

> **HOW TO MAKE THE MAGIC:** Ask everyone in your family how they would like to help other people. What really tugs at them? It could be helping to stamp out homelessness in your city or relieve hunger in Africa. Or it could be even closer to home, like putting an end to bullying at school. All that matters is that they are motivated by kindness. Give them a couple of weeks to think about it, then meet again and decide where you will focus your energy to make a difference—and to give love a fighting chance. My own hope is that love will become the weapon of the future and replace hate in the heart of every child. But perhaps more immediately, I hope that this approach will help you, as a parent, understand that we do not have a perfect world. Maybe this awareness will help you find peace related to all the day-to-day things you cannot fix—and help you see how insignificant some of those "imperfections" really are.

LIVING IN THE MOMENT

It isn't the experience of today that drives men mad. It is the remorse.
For something that happened yesterday, and the dread of what
tomorrow may bring.

—ROBERT JONES BURDETTE

. . . .

Young children and animals live in the moment; parents and adults worry about the future. When you spend too much time fretting about what may happen and distressing over the events far in advance, you forget to enjoy the moment that you are in.

The night our twins were born, I sat up into the wee hours of the morning working on my finances. As I mentioned at the beginning of this book, I calculated that since I had five children, all born within seven years of each other, I would be paying tuition for all of them at the same time as they went to college and graduate school. I sat there going over numbers that seemed impossible for me to ever achieve, and by 2:00 a.m. I was feeling a bit harried, to put it mildly. At that point I suddenly remembered the twins weren't even one day old yet, and I was already worrying about what was twenty years into the future. I laughed, took a break, and eventually fell asleep. When the actual time came, they didn't follow my worrisome schedule and predictions, which helped a lot; and with loans and good fortune, we made it through those years.

Don't spend so much time worrying about things that may or may not happen because most of them never happen. You will miss the seconds, minutes, hours, and days you have right now and here with your family. You cannot predict the future, so don't overprepare for it! You only create troubles by getting ready for what may never happen.

HOW TO MAKE THE MAGIC: Make a list of your worries, and then ask yourself how worrying solves any of the problems you have listed. Now tear up the list and go and enjoy the day. Remember you can either spend your lifetime worrying or spend it living. Which would you prefer for yourself and your loved ones?

TAKE A PARENTING
VACATION

I love people. I love my family, my children . . . but inside myself
is a place where I live all alone and that's where you renew your springs
that never dry up.

—Pearl S. Buck

. . . .

As a parent, you may find that your children's needs always seem to come first. But when the children are taken care of, what do you do to care for yourself? My wife and I often developed illnesses while caring for our five young children. I realized that as parents we can deplete ourselves and suffer the consequences. There are stress factors called life crisis units, and the more of them you accumulate, the more likely you are to become sick.

Noticing our exhaustion, my wife, Bobbie, and I came up with a solution that really helped us to meet our needs. Every January, Bobbie would take out the calendar and draw a line through one week in every season. She always knew just how long we could go before the stress took its toll. During those weeks, Bobbie and I would take a vacation, just the two of us without the five children, and have time together to share the experience of life instead of being caught up in who had to do what today. Those weeks helped us to survive and, I am sure, helped our marriage and relationship as well.

We had other times when the whole family went away together, including the pets, kids, and their friends. These were wonderful, too, but we did not let them replace the alone time we needed for our own self-care.

I also remember attending a workshop during that time to learn how to help my patients deal with loss. What I didn't expect was that I would end up learning an important parenting lesson, too. Each participant shared stories about their losses, but when my turn came, I shared about my anger at all the things I felt responsible for at home and at work and how unfair it all seemed. This was when Elisabeth Kübler-Ross looked at me and said, "You have needs, too." That sentence stayed with me and has helped me ever since, both as a parent and as a doctor.

HOW TO MAKE THE MAGIC: Grab the calendar and mark off some parental vacation time when you and your spouse can get away alone together. Use this time to enjoy each other's presence and discuss things other than the problems related to raising your children. If you can't take a week, start with a dinner, a day, or a weekend away. If you are a single parent, arrange for a babysitter and take some time alone, or attend a workshop, or go off on some adventure with a friend.

LOVE, MAGIC & MUDPIES

LET YOUR AGE BE AN ASSET

And in the end, it's not the years in your life that count.
It's the life in your years.

—Abraham Lincoln

• • • •

We no longer live in a time when families are expected to look like the one in *Leave it to Beaver* or *Father Knows Best,* with a thirtysomething father who puts on a suit and goes to work every day while his twentysomething wife stays home in a cute little dress and bakes cookies for her two incredibly wholesome boys. Today anything goes, especially when it comes to age. Many parents start to have kids when in their forties, while others start families in their teens.

If you're anything like me, your chronological age has nothing to do with how young you feel or what you are capable of doing; but as a parent, you need to recognize that being an older or a younger parent is still slightly off the norm. Children benefit from the wisdom and experience that older parents have to offer, yet they may sometimes feel deprived if you can't keep up with the younger parents or don't want to participate in some of their activities. Younger parents may have more energy and be a little more "hip" than some older parents, yet they may lack life experience and maturity because they are still children themselves in many ways.

Don't let your parental age be a handicap. Just be the parent that you want to be and that your child needs you to be, regardless of how old or young you are. Team up with other parents and learn from their experience. Join a parents' group. Take classes through your local adult learning center. You won't just learn how to be a good parent, you'll also learn how to teach your children how to appreciate the parent you already are.

Focus on the positive gifts you bring to your kids because of your age. If you are an older parent, awaken your child to what you have learned from your experience that younger parents may not be aware of. For example, if you lost your hair due to chemotherapy and attend Open School Day, don't be upset by your child's reaction to a parent who looks different. Help him or her learn to respect you for the wisdom you have accumulated rather than being angry because you are different from most of the other kids' parents due to age or health problems. If you are a younger parent, emphasize how much fun you have playing with your children and how much you can relate to them because of your own youth.

Most of all, just love your children, no matter what age you are as a parent, and they will thrive. A healthy family accepts one another for who they are rather than resenting them for who they aren't.

How to Make the Magic: Pick a Saturday to switch roles with your kids, for a day or even a few hours. They will be the parents and you will be the kids. Set basic ground rules to ensure safety, discuss your options, and then go about your day in each other's shoes. Afterward, sit down and talk about how you felt, what you learned, and what, if anything, you would like to change.

UNDERSTAND WHY

A mother understands what a child does not say.

—Jewish Proverb

. . . .

All parents occasionally get hurt feelings over things their children say or do. Many times we wouldn't be offended at all if we understood what our children had in mind, but often we do not even ask them. One weekend my wife and I planned to stop to visit our son, Keith, and his family on our way to Cape Cod. We had car trouble, so we didn't leave until an hour or so later than expected. Naturally, I called Keith to tell him we would be late. When we arrived at his house, he came out to greet us, but when I said that we needed to come in and use his bathroom, he told us he was sorry but we could not come in. I was too stunned to argue or question him. I knew we were late, but his reaction seemed excessively punishing. I felt disturbed and hurt that entire day and evening. The next day I called to vent my anger and tell him how I felt about how he had treated us. When I told him I was upset by his not letting us in, he explained that his mother-in-law was sick; she was asleep on their living room couch. His wife and son were also sick; they were sleeping upstairs. He felt that if we had come in, we would have awakened them. When I heard his explanation, I understood his behavior and no longer felt I had been mistreated. The anger and hurt I had felt were gone. My ability to understand his decision changed my feelings and reaction. Even if I hadn't agreed with the way he handled the situation, the fact that I was able to understand why he did it alleviated my feelings of rejection or abuse.

How to Make the Magic: Consider something one of your children did recently or in the past that upset you. Surely you wondered why he or she acted in that way. Give yourself time to relax and feel composed. Sit down with a cup of tea and some soothing music. Take a walk. Read a favorite magazine. It doesn't matter what you do as long as it makes you feel at ease. When you are composed and your emotions are under control, sit down with your child and ask why she did what she did. Tell her you are not judging her action but just want to understand. You may be surprised at how much better both of you will feel.

PAINT THERAPY

I was not out to paint beautiful pictures; even painting good pictures was not important to me. I wanted only to help the truth burst forth.

—ALICE MILLER

• • • •

One of the best therapies I have found to relax myself and escape family problems is painting. You may have no artistic talents, but I am going to insist you paint a portrait of your children with a paintbrush. It can be in any situation, from an outdoor picnic to a picture of your kids sleeping in bed. I want you to look at them in a way you have never seen them before.

Let your creativity flow. Let your painting show the world who your family really is and what is special about them. So what do you see when you look at your child? How much more than a child do you see? What you will notice is that all the tension will begin to drain away as you focus on your painting and new perspective. One of my portraits is called "Jeffrey and Friends" because it shows our son surrounded by various pets and animals. He is more than just a person because of all the relationships he has and lives he has touched.

Start making notes about your children until you feel you can really see who they are, and then sit down and compose a portrait. When you feel ready to share your art with others, show it to the subject in question, and then display it for all to see who enter your home.

HOW TO MAKE THE MAGIC: You are not going to get out of this one by saying you are not an artist. Your family is your blank canvas and easel, and you are to make them into a work of art. Do it now!

TIME OUT

You may occasionally overhear a mother say, "Children must have their naps. It's Mother who knows best." When what she really means by that is that she needs a rest.

—Donna Evleth

. . . .

I t's stylish for parents to shout "Time out!" when their kids are driving them crazy. Then everyone is sent to their room for a certain time interval to cool off and quiet down.

But what would happen if you took time out for yourself, not only to free you from the exhaustion associated with parenting and feeling overwhelmed, but just to give you some pleasant and peaceful moments during the day? Having personal time will help you to restore and refresh yourself so that you can enjoy being a parent.

What if whenever you shouted "Time out!" the children knew you were going to retreat into a space that was your sanctuary, which is what I call white room time. Right now think about sitting in a totally white room with no windows or decorations of any sort. How would you feel? If you find it boring and want to decorate it, then your energy level is probably okay and you can keep going. However, if you find the absence of stimulation peaceful and are glad for the opportunity to rest, then start yelling "Time out!" for yourself and tell the kids you are going into your white room.

Soon your children will begin to understand your need to care for yourself and that the "white room" really just represents your private space. This will encourage your children to respect others; they'll realize that everyone has individual needs and that they need to show the same consideration for others as they do for themselves.

> **HOW TO MAKE THE MAGIC:** Find a space in your home or apartment where you can create a sanctuary or white room. Pick the right music and lighting, even construct an altar with items that will help replenish your body, spirit, and soul. Then let everyone know its purpose and that when you are going there, you will call "Time out!" or "White room time!" Be sure they know that everyone in the family is entitled to this time and can use the room when feeling stressed or just in need of some quiet time.

YOUR CANDLE

It's better to burn brightly for half as long than to be a dim lingering light.

—ROLAND GIFT

. . . .

Everyone should think of their life as a candle. The length of the candle is not about your age but how much lifetime you have left to live and how well you live it.

The point I want to make is that you should not be living a life that will lead your candle to burn out before your time. You need to live a life that allows you to burn brightly with the energy and joy of what you are experiencing.

Now, how do you know which one you are doing? Are you burning up brightly or burning out?

There is one simple test that will tell you. The next time you feel tired, take a nap. If, when you wake up, you are feeling rested, restored, and ready to go, you are burning up and the physical rest restored you. If you are burning out, you will awaken with the same sense of fatigue you had when you lay down to take your nap. If this is the case, your problem is more than just physical; it is emotional and you need more than a rest to correct it. You need a change in your lifestyle.

Take time to assess your needs and check your candle flame often to be sure it is burning brightly.

> **HOW TO MAKE THE MAGIC:** Watch for the signs of burnout. When your body and mind are constantly stressed, it is easy to get extremely fatigued. Burnout is a physical, mental, and emotional response to constant levels of high stress. Burnout can make you feel hopeless, resentful, and depressed. Check into the different types of techniques that can help you develop better coping skills, including mental imagery/visualization, positive self-talk, and biofeedback. You might consider finding a professional such as a therapist or life coach to help you hone these skills.

EMPTY NEST

When mothers talk about the depression of the empty nest, they're
not mourning the passing of all those wet towels on the floor, or the music
that numbs your teeth, or even the bottle of capless shampoo dribbling
down the shower drain. They're upset because they've gone from
supervisor of a child's life to a spectator. It's like being the vice president
of the United States.

—ERMA BOMBECK

• • • •

There is a time when all baby birds must leave the nest. But they won't be able to fly if you don't provide them with training and help prepare them for the world out there. One of the hardest jobs you have to do is prepare yourself for the time when one of your children leaves home. Up until then, most of your time, effort, and energy will be spent parenting your young ones. Along the way, it is important to take care of your own needs as well. When I was a young man, I never lived alone, and so when our teenagers set off across the country on their own, I was very proud of them. I enjoyed listening to the problems they were having and saw the many different ways they were learning to take on responsibility. When they lived at home, everything had been *my* problem, even when they destroyed their rooms with their activities, hobbies, and pets. Now they had to take care of their own messes and pay the repair bills.

So take a deep breath, and let go. It is one of the most meaningful gifts you can give your children. Be there when they ask for help, cheer them on, but let them learn the life lessons they need to so they can grow as adults. This includes allowing them to make mistakes and encouraging them to keep trying so they never feel like failures.

When the nest is empty, their spirit and love will still remain, even though you may feel the absence of their touch and presence. Now is the time when you have to think about what you need to get in touch with in your life. People everywhere on this planet could use your help, but it is neither for me nor your family to tell you what to do when the nest is empty and who your next family should be.

One clue I will mention. Notice that mama and papa birds don't stay in the nest after the kids leave. Don't spend too much time moping around; get off your butt and stop feeling sorry for yourself. Get out there in the world. Go to school. Get a fun job. Volunteer. Write poetry or books. Sign up for an art class. Take up a sport. Run a marathon, and raise money to cure something. Learn yoga or martial arts. And if you don't know what to do now that they are gone, that becomes the next problem for you to solve.

LOVE, MAGIC & MUDPIES

How to Make the Magic: Whether your kids are gone or not, act as if they are and get involved in some activity, so when the nest is empty, you'll be happy to have the free time to pursue these interests. I can remember how my mom worried about my dad when my younger sister went off to college. The day my sister left, my dad told my mom how glad he was that they would both have more time for themselves. She felt much better after that. Just think of all the time and energy you will now have to devote to your interests, hobbies, and other relationships. Now it's time for *you*!

YOUR MIRACULOUS FAMILY

If you want to make a difference and create a world where we can begin to live in peace, your responsibility as a parent is to raise your children with love, kindness, conscious awareness, and compassion. When you raise a loved child whose body and soul are primed to respond to positive touch, feelings, and emotions, you are helping to make the world a more loving place for us all.

Please understand that when you raise a loving child, you are also creating the landscape that will influence what he or she becomes as an adult. From that landscape, your child can either grow wild and uncontrollable like a weed, blotting out life in other living things, or he can blossom into a gorgeous flower, spreading seeds of love to beautify the world with kindness.

We need to wake up as parents and teach our children the importance of kindness; we need to empower them to know they can make a difference. If you want to end wars and aggression, raise a child who knows he is loved. When he's playing, his energy will enhance teamwork and not express violence. His aggression will be used to build homes, not destroy them.

When every child grows up loved, the world will see an end to wars, global warming, pollution, starvation, and every self-destructive behavior you can think of, both on a personal level and in society. Love is the ultimate weapon that will save us all. Teach your children to take action, so we won't wake up and realize we are faced with the reality of the end of life on our planet. As a physician, I see individuals who, when they learn their lives are threatened by a disease, start to live a new life based upon love and not material things. Let's not wait.

The torch is now in your hands. Pass it on to your children and have them carry it on and enlighten the world.

As you think over what you've read, I ask only one thing of you: Please create a list of all the things you believe are required to create loving parents and families. When you complete the list, see how many things you can honestly say you do. Give yourself credit where you deserve it, and be honest where you can see you are lacking. Then, begin to live the message you have created.

Remember, this whole crazy enterprise is about becoming the parent you want to be and creating the child you want to create. It is never too late. Start today.

> The child must know that he is a miracle, that since the beginning of the world there hasn't been, and until the end of the world there will not be, another child like him.

> —PABLO CASALS